WALKING FOR WEIGHT-LOSS

WALKING FOR WEIGHT-LOSS

The Easy Way to Slim Down and Tone Up

LUCY KNIGHT

BARNES & NOBLE
NEW YORK

This 2007 edition published by Barnes & Noble, Inc. by arrangement with Kyle Cathie Ltd.

ISBN-13: 978 0 7607 8667 3
ISBN-10: 0 7607 8667 4

Project editor: Vicki Murrell
Copy editor: Morag Lyall
Proofreader: Ruth Baldwin
Design: Caroline and Roger Hillier,
The Old Chapel Graphic Design
Production: Sha Huxtable and Alice Holloway

Printed and bound in Singapore by KHL

1 3 5 7 9 10 8 6 4 2

Contents

Introduction

Most of us want to slim down and improve our level of fitness, but these days there are so many exercise options and the potential for so much confusion. Is it really necessary to pay that costly gym membership; and if we listen to one expert, does that mean the other is wrong? The problem is that they are all mostly right, and we are presented with an off-putting array of choices. However, the solution is staring us in the face as there is an activity that we do every day, which is as natural as breathing and that can provide the key to safe, sustainable weight-loss we can even enjoy. . . . WALKING.

Most of us have been walking since about the time of our first or second birthday. It is beneficial for all ages, free, and lifts our mood simply by getting us out in the fresh air, so why on earth don't we do it more? Unfortunately, most of us are tied to our desk all day; we jump into our car to travel anywhere that's farther than the local stores; and now it's hardly necessary to do even that as we can buy almost anything we need—even groceries—online. But, if we want to transform our sedentary lifestyle, walking is a very good place to start.

So can we really lose weight through walking? The answer is yes. We just need to take a look at our technique, speed up our pace, and change our focus. In this book I will show you easy ways to ensure just that, by providing programs with clear, attainable goals so that you can assess your progress and make sure you are improving all the time. Although I focus mainly on "power walking," I also discuss the many other styles of walking that you can try, as well as ideas for how you can increase your daily activity by incorporating general walking into your everyday routine.

Of course, as always with weight-loss, exercise and diet do go hand in hand, and it's no good walking for three miles and then eating a jelly doughnut as a snack. I have therefore provided essential guidelines for a healthy diet and how to achieve a balance, so that you're not always fighting those cravings. In fact you will be amazed at how easy and enjoyable this new, active lifestyle can be.

The great thing about walking is that you already know how to do it; and even if you haven't taken part in any exercise for a long time, it's unlikely that you'll be too out of practice! So whatever level you start at, you can slowly build up pace, distance, and technique and, regardless of age, fitness level, or experience, reap the benefits. Walking is the perfect exercise for achieving not only weight-loss, but complete mental and physical health, as well as a new zest for life. So what are you waiting for?

> ***Even the longest journey begins with a single step***
>
> Chinese proverb

Why power walk?

Researchers in the field of sports and fitness have described walking as "the nearest activity to perfect exercise." At first glance, it seems far too simplistic to claim that a basic skill that most of us do without a second thought can be significant, but as you learn more about your body and the benefits of walking you will realize that it is true: the action of walking may be simple, but the results for your health and daily living are far-reaching.

Walking briskly, with a high arm swing is the simple and easy way to shed those unwanted pounds and enjoy a fitter and trimmer figure. It provides a low-impact but also vigorous and well-rounded fitness activity that will significantly speed up your metabolism and boost your calorie-burning potential. And weight-loss is just one of the many benefits that goes hand in hand with regular walking, as it will also increase your energy levels, improve your level of fitness and lead to better health.

Life is no fun if every day is a battle to find your energy and sparkle. Exercise in any shape or form is vital to your wellbeing and it's important that you make time for it, and do something that you enjoy. Getting started with your power walking program will not be a burden on you or on those around you, and it certainly won't break the bank. It's free, easy and extremely sociable, so why not start it **TODAY**?

WHY WALK?

We used to be so much fitter, and thinner. In the days before cars and public transportation, we had to walk to get wherever we needed to go. Even in quite recent years it was common for children to walk to school; their leisure time was spent outside, walking, running, and chasing around, rather than glued in front of a computer; and adults generally had far less sedentary jobs and owned only one car per household.

In this modern world it is hard to get the exercise we need without pursuing it as an extra activity in our day. It shouldn't have to be this way—we should be able to sustain a healthy weight and fitness level through an active lifestyle. But as our children sit in front of the television and we become more and more dependent on our personal computers, it is clear that we need a new and practical approach.

Even though all my work is based in areas of fitness and dance, I sometimes notice that days have gone by when I have simply gotten up, climbed into my car, and driven to work, sat in front of my computer, and then driven home and sprawled on the sofa for the whole evening. I'm sure we can all relate to that. If it weren't for the extra activity that we choose to fit into our life, weeks, months, even years could go by without our needing to be in any way physical. We're all battling surplus fat and the problems associated with it—heart disease, high blood pressure, diabetes, osteoarthritis, poor energy levels, and low self-esteem—and therefore we have to make a conscious choice to be fit and active. To lose weight and keep it off, we need to get moving, and power walking provides us with the ideal solution.

Power walking

Power walking is the perfect choice for weight-loss, as its aerobic demands are similar to those of a running program and yet it's much, much kinder on your body, with about 50 percent less impact and wear and tear on your joints. It also provides you with a challenging cardiovascular workout that will quickly improve muscle tone in your entire lower body—bottom, thighs, hips, and abs—as well as upper back and shoulders.

When you power walk, you generally move along at a brisk pace of 4½–6 mph (7–9.5 kph), covering 1 mile (1.6 kilometers) in 10–13.6 minutes. It is very important that you keep up a good speed as this is one of the crucial factors that will determine the intensity of your workout and maximize your fat-burning potential. By working at 60–70% of your maximum heart rate (all explained on page 92) your body will turn to its fat stores to provide the necessary energy and build muscle, which in turn raises your basal metabolic rate so that you are burning calories all day long.

When walking at a normal pace, women average around 3mph and men a slightly faster 3.5mph. Power walking requires you to almost double this and in the process, significantly raises the aerobic challenge. If you want to lose weight and tone up without being a slave to the gym, power walking is the obvious answer; you even get to enjoy the advantages of fresh air and the great outdoors. Here are just some of the benefits of taking up power walking. . . .

Weight-loss

As with any sustained physical activity, walking will cause your metabolism to burn calories, converting carbohydrates, fats, and proteins into energy, rather than storing them as body fat. Weight is dependent on the simple equation of calories consumed versus calories burned, and weight gain is almost always down to an imbalance in this equation. If you increase the number of calories you burn each day through exercise, the weight should drop off.

However, walking is not only going to burn fat, as it will also increase the muscle mass in your body as you tone up. This is a key factor in weight-loss because muscle burns more calories than fat does; therefore the more muscle you have in relation to fat, the higher your basal metabolic rate (BMR) will be, the minimum amount of energy your body requires to function on a daily basis. Also, losing the fat and gaining more muscle will reshape those thighs, bottom, tummy, and upper body—which will all be a big part of the new you.

In order to get good results from your *Walking for Weight-Loss* program, you must be aware of how hard you are working. You need to start off at a pace and duration that suit your fitness level, for it's no good being reasonably fit and sauntering down the road at a pace that doesn't even raise your temperature. Although any walking is good exercise, if you are aiming to lose weight, for intensity is important, as you need to encourage your body to use fat as fuel (I discuss this in more detail later in the book; see pages 89–97).

The ideal way to lose weight is always through a combination of exercise and diet. One without the other can bring some results, but will never be as effective as a double-targeted approach. As a unified program, walking combined with healthy eating will help you reduce your weight at a sensible and sustainable pace and improve your body shape, giving your muscles a toned and enviably streamlined look.

Regular walking helps fight disease

Researchers at the University of South Carolina and the University of Massachusetts recently studied some 550 adults. Those who regularly exercised at least moderately had about 25 percent fewer colds during the one-year study than those who seldom or never exercised. Results of at least three small clinical trials tend to confirm that finding. In all three, women who were told to walk briskly most days for three months developed colds only about half as often as those who didn't exercise.

A healthy immune system

Walking doesn't merely help you lose weight; as being in a fit and healthy condition will also help protect you against infection and disease. Physical activity increases your heart rate, strengthens your heart, and increases blood circulation through your body, bringing more oxygen and nutrients to your organs.

Therefore, if you raise your activity by walking, the increased oxygen supply will stimulate your immune system, repairing any damaged tissue and protecting against diseases and free radicals. And when your heart and lungs become more efficient at transporting blood and oxygen around the body, you will also find that your fitness level increases very swiftly. This means you will not get out of breath as quickly once you start moving, and you will generally feel more able to continue exercising for longer periods of time.

Walking is a good way of managing stress levels, too, making it easier for you to sleep at night, which is also essential for a healthy immune system. Even one sleepless night can significantly suppress the immune system, and therefore it follows that the more exercise you do, the more you will benefit. However, it is also important to note that while your fitness program should always provide you with a challenge, it is not a good idea to push yourself to the point of exhaustion or overdo it when you are feeling unwell, as this will certainly stress your immune system and leave you run down.

Regular walking can also greatly increase your chances of maintaining a healthy heart. In fact recent research suggests that it can cut your chances of a heart attack by as much as 50 percent. As with any aerobic exercise, it will strengthen and improve the efficiency of the heart and circulation and reduce high blood pressure and high cholesterol levels. And, of course, by losing weight you will also reduce the heart's workload.

Beating breast cancer

A study performed by Dr. Michelle Holmes of Brigham Women's Hospital, Boston, followed 3,000 breast cancer patients, tracking their health and exercise habits for up to 18 years. The results showed that women with breast cancer who walked for 3–5 hours per week were 50 percent more likely to survive their diagnoses compared to inactive women with breast cancer.

A walk a day keeps a stroke away

A study by Frank B. Hu, M.D., Ph.D., which was published in the *Journal of the American Medical Association*, included more than 70,000 female nurses in their 40s, 50s, and 60s. Those who walked at a moderate pace on most days of the week for at least 30 minutes reduced their risk of ischemic stroke, the most common type, by about 20 percent. Those who walked at a brisk pace or very brisk pace reduced their risk by about 40 percent.

Joint and bone health

If we want to live a long and independent life, we must maintain the condition of our joints and bones, for crippling conditions such as osteoporosis and arthritis can be a major reason why elderly people stop managing alone. Osteoporosis, or "brittle bone disease," weakens bones to the point where they break easily—most often in the hip, spine, and wrist. It is also called the silent disease for you may have been losing bone strength for years, but do not become aware of it until a bone breaks.

Walking is a weight-bearing exercise and is therefore an essential tool in the battle against osteoporosis, as it maintains bone density. Bones are like muscles in the way that they get stronger and denser the more demands you place on them. The pull of a muscle against a bone, together with the force of gravity while walking, stresses the bone, which responds by stimulating tissue growth and renewal. Unfortunately, weakening bones are a fact of life that everyone, especially women, must face as they grow older. The good news is that regular walking is the best prevention and also the best form of treatment.

The other great thing about walking is that while it is a weight-bearing exercise it is not high impact, like jogging. Therefore it strengthens and stabilizes the muscles around your major joints but reduces the amount of wear and tear on the cartilage (the cause of osteoarthritis). Medical experts agree that exercise plays a vital role in maintaining bone and joint health. It also helps to maintain muscle strength, agility, mobility, and flexibility. So get walking. . . .

Improving posture and back pain

How you hold your body is very important for walking comfortably and easily. With good posture, you will be able to breathe more easily and also avoid back pain, which is the most prevalent cause of disability in people under the age of 45.

The problem is that it is all too easy for bad posture to creep in. On a daily basis, we often find ourselves slumped over our PC, flopping on the sofa at home, or driving the car hunched over the steering wheel. And even when we stand for long periods it's rarely without something to lean against. Our backs are therefore weak, and we have forgotten how to use our postural muscles to give our bodies integral support. Later in the book I cover postural exercises (see pages 24–35) that will show you how to correct bad habits.

Our bodies are designed with balance in mind, so if your posture is incorrect you are placing added stress on the parts of your body that have to compensate in order to keep you upright. With the techniques of the walking program, you will initially have to make a conscious effort to maintain good posture, but it will soon become second nature to you.

Back sufferers sometimes feel reluctant to try exercising for fear of making their pain worse. However, if you start gently then walking will strengthen the core muscles (the the deep abdominal and lower back muscles running right around the middle of your body like a corset) and, when correctly engaged will go a long way to prevent further injury.

Exercise for the mind

Walking is not just physical exercise for the body; it's also great exercise for the mind. Have you ever noticed how sluggish your mind becomes when you go for too long without doing something physically energetic? Being outside in the fresh air, in beautiful surroundings, really will blow away the cobwebs, allowing time for clear thinking and inducing a relaxed state (even meditative; see page 112). Getting out in nature is great for the mind, body, and spirit.

For people suffering from depression or a stress-related illness, walking 3 or 4 times a week for 30 minutes has been shown to have a positive effect on mood and self-esteem. Through vigorous walking, the body releases proteins called endorphins, which are a natural antidepressant and which lift our mood and give us the feel-good factor that we experience after a good workout. In fact, studies performed by James Blumenthal, a professor of medical psychology at Duke University in Durham, North Carolina, show that "exercise, at least when performed in a group setting, seems to be at least as effective as standard antidepressant medications in reducing symptoms in patients with major depression. . . .duration of exercise didn't seem to matter—what seemed to matter most was whether people were exercising or not."

People who are more physically fit tend to have fewer stress-related health problems. When they exercise regularly, they are likely to have fewer symptoms of depression, such as trouble sleeping at night, sleeping too

much during the day, overeating, or not eating at all. Lack of sleep can be a big problem for people suffering with anxiety or depression; and just by achieving a better quality of sleep, you can feel calmer and more able to cope with the day ahead.

Walking regularly can have such a positive effect on your life that you would scarcely believe it could be so simple. You will feel better about your body shape, be more able to deal with stressful situations, and, most important, have done something really positive for yourself, which will have a good impact on all areas of your life.

Improving your social life

There are many ways in which you can use walking to improve your social life. Finding the time to walk with friends and family can really nurture relationships, and a long, brisk walk on a Sunday afternoon has a way of initiating new conversations and forging new bonds. It's also a great way to get all the family out together and incredibly beneficial for children and teenagers who have got into the habit of spending all their time indoors.

If you are walking alone, go to an area where there are other walkers/joggers or walk around your local district. Not only is it safer, but you will increase your chances of bumping into a neighbor or someone you know. There are also many walking groups all over the country that you could join. These are a fantastic opportunity to get fit and perhaps even get involved in a charity fundraiser or competition.

Financial benefit

Walking won't drain your finances in the same way that other hobbies do. It requires no costly gym membership or equipment, other than a good pair of running shoes, and it guarantees you a great workout in the fresh air, all for free!

Emotional benefits at a glance

Increases energy levels	**Increases alertness**
Lifts the mood	**Relieves premenstrual symptoms**
Reduces stress	**Improves self-esteem**
Aids sleep	**Can be a sociable experience**

Physical benefits at a glance

- Reduces the risk of heart disease
- Reduces the risk of a stroke
- Can reduce the risk of some types of cancer
- Reduces the risk of type 2 diabetes
- Lowers high blood pressure
- Builds bone density, reducing the chances of developing osteoporosis
- Strengthens joints and muscles
- Reduces body fat
- Improves body shape
- Increases fitness level
- Reduces bad (LDL) cholesterol levels
- Improves flexibility
- Can improve arthritis
- Improves posture
- Reduces back pain
- Boosts the immune system

POSTURE CHECK

CHAPTER 2

Your posture projects to the outside world who you are and how you are feeling. In fact, it says so much about you that it could be the difference between your getting a job. . . .or not! Poor posture often makes you appear a lot less confident than you really are and can actually make you look a good bit heavier. If you learn to hold yourself well, you will look slimmer and seem more approachable – it's got to be worth a try!

Correct posture is all about maintaining each part of the body in its proper alignment, whether standing, sitting, or lying down. Unfortunately, bad posture is a sign of our twenty-first-century lifestyle, since most of us spend our day slouching in one way or another, and therefore our postural muscles are weak from lack of use.

Good posture is a very simple but hugely important factor in keeping the back and spine healthy, and therefore avoiding back pain later in life. A recent buzz phrase in the fitness industry is "core strength" which means working on the corset-like muscles of the abdominals and lower back that support our center. When they contract, they stabilize the spine, pelvis, and shoulders and so create a solid center of support, which acts as a foundation for all movement. If we are to correct our posture, the first thing we must do is strengthen these muscles and reverse years of bad habits. In this chapter I have devised a routine to improve your core stability and strengthen the whole torso. It will greatly assist your walking technique and also be invaluable in your everyday activities.

To make sure you maintain correct posture when walking, you must first be able to sustain it when not moving, so let's have a look at how you find your correct posture in different stationary positions. . . .

Finding correct posture

Engaging your core

The first important thing is to learn how to engage your core muscles, as these will provide you with a solid base for movement. Your spine curves in naturally at the neck (cervical spine), then out at the upper back (thoracic spine) and in again at the lower back (lumbar spine). These natural curves are designed to absorb any shock or impact going through your body, but they must be neutrally aligned with the pelvis and not exaggerated. This is where your abdominal muscles come into play, for, once they are engaged, it is almost impossible for the curves to become exaggerated and exert unnecessary pressure on the spine. Try the following exercise.

1 In a standing position, feet parallel and hip width apart, first allow your tummy to relax.

2 Then focus on the muscles between your pelvis and the bottom of your rib cage and think of them as a corset that, when tightened, stops your pelvis from moving in and out of its neutral position. To tighten it, imagine that you are pulling your navel in towards your spine while drawing up your pelvic floor muscles (these are the muscles you would use to stop yourself on the toilet in mid-flow). It may help to take one hand to your lower back (palm away) and the other to your tummy (palm touching). You should feel the tummy draw away from the front hand while the back remains still (not pressing into the hand behind).

3 Hold for 5 seconds initially, and repeat regularly throughout the day so you feel comfortable with this position. This is what I want you to do each time I ask you to engage your core.

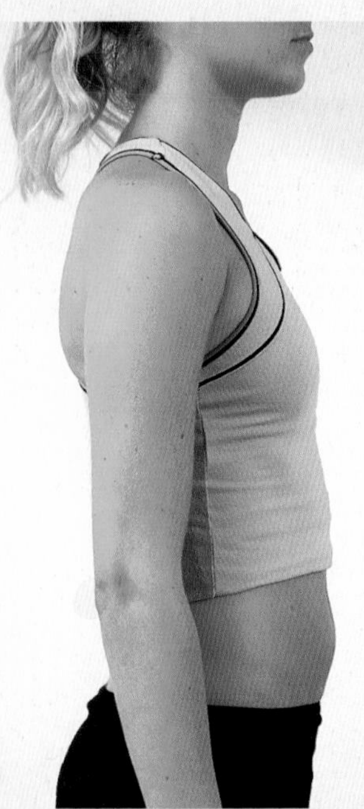

1

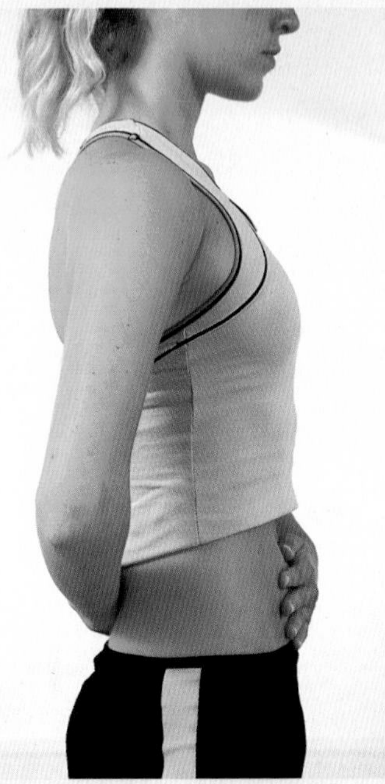

2

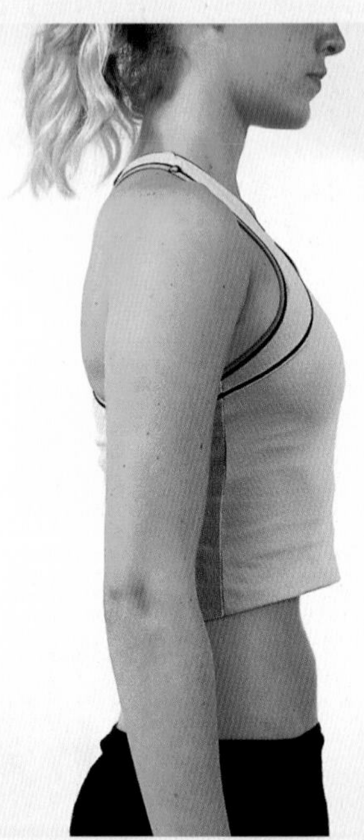

3

Correct standing posture

1 Stand with your feet parallel and hip width apart. Make sure that your knees and pelvis are slightly softened, and your shoulders are back and down. Tuck your chin in so that your ears are in line with your shoulders, and focus on something straight ahead at eye level. Engage your core by pulling your navel in toward your spine

2 Now rock your body forward by transferring your weight onto your toes.

3 Then rock back, taking your weight onto your heels. The aim is to find your standing center of balance, so keep rocking forward and back, gradually making the movement smaller and smaller until you find the center point where your weight feels evenly distributed between your toes and your heels.

Spend a moment in this position, and remember how it feels so that you can come back to it easily each time you are standing.

2

3

Correct sitting posture

Sit on a hard-backed chair, with your hips pressed as far against the back as possible. Make sure that your feet and knees are hip width apart and your knees and hips are level. Check that your back is straight and your ears, shoulders, and hips are all in line. If you have a full-length mirror, set the chair in front of it so you can check your alignment and get used to feeling the position.

Engage your core by pulling your navel in toward your spine. Check that your lower back is not over-arched or completely flat but somewhere in between. Spend a few moments in this position, and make a mental note of how it feels so that you can come back to it easily next time you are seated.

Correct lying posture

Lie on your back with your knees bent and feet flat on the floor. Rest your arms by your sides, and check that your chin is not sticking out. Relax your pelvis and feel its contact with the floor. Check that you are not flattening or over-arching your lower back—feel the natural curve of the spine (there should be just enough space to slide a piece of paper underneath).

Engage your core. Now imagine that there is a piece of string attached to the crown of your head, pulling away from your body and lengthening your spine. You should feel as if you are growing taller. Make sure that your shoulders are rolled back so that they are in line with your ears, and press the entire length of your arms firmly into the floor. Hold this position for a little while, remembering how it feels for the next time.

Good posture in the office

Back support
Make sure that your office chair has good back support. You should sit with your bottom at the back of the chair, and the curve of the chair should fit into the curve of your lower back. Adjust the chair until it fits you properly.

Chair height
Your chair should have adjustable height. Sit with your feet flat on the floor, and your knees and hips should be in line. Never have your hips lower than your knees, as this will put considerable strain on the lower back.

Computer position
Your computer monitor and keyboard should be directly in front of you when you are working. Never put them in a position where you need constantly to look or twist one way or the other.

Forearm position
You should sit at a height that enables you to rest your forearms on the desk comfortably. The keyboard should be close to the level of your elbows, so that you don't have to raise or lower them too much when you type. Try to keep neutral alignment in the wrists, as this will guard against repetitive strain; you may find that resting them on a computer pad helps.

Posture exercises

By stretching and strengthening, the following exercises will help give you more control and stability in your core muscles and more flexibility and motion overall.

1 CHIN TUCK

What for?

This exercise is great for correcting an over-extended neck and aligning the head with the rest of the spine. Take a look at yourself in old photographs and see if you have a habit of jutting your chin forward. Many of us are guilty of this, and it is often the root cause of headaches and tension in the neck and shoulders.

How to do it

Either sitting or standing tall, place one finger on your chin and gently guide your chin and head backwards until your neck is in line with your shoulders. Hold the position for 10 seconds and then relax.

1

How many? Repeat up to 10 times.

Top tips

• Try catching your reflection in a mirror out of the corner of your eye when performing this exercise.
• Focus on something at eye level so you are not tempted to tilt your chin upward.

2 DOORWAY CHEST STRETCH

What for?

This stretch will open out the muscles in the chest, which often become tight, consequently pulling the shoulders forward and creating a hunched stance.

How to do it

a Stand in an open doorway and, with your elbows bent at right angles, place your hands each side of the door frame.

b Step the right foot forward and bend the knee, taking your weight forward onto the right leg. Bend the knee until you feel a stretch across the front of your chest. Hold the stretch for 30 seconds.

How many? Repeat 2–4 times on each side.

Top tips

• Don't allow your back to arch as you lunge forward.
• Increase the intensity of the stretch by bending the front knee more.
• Take the stretch only as far as feels comfortable.

2a

2b

3b

3 WALL ARM RAISE

What for?
This exercise will open up the chest and work the muscles in your upper back. It should give you a great sense of standing up tall and an idea of correct alignment in the upper back and shoulder area.

How to do it
a Stand with your back against a wall and your feet hip width apart. Bend your arms at right angles, and place them against the wall with your elbows at shoulder level.

b Slowly slide your arms up the wall until your elbows are level with your ears, and then lower them back down again. Make sure your lower back is pressed into the wall and your elbows and wrists remain in contact with the wall throughout the movement.

How many? Repeat 10 times.

Top tips
- Keep the movement slow and controlled all the way through.
- Check that your body is straight and still, with the only movement coming from the arms.
- Do not allow your back to arch as your arms move up and down.

4 SEATED ABDOMINAL EXERCISE

What for?
This teaches you how to "hold your center."

How to do it
Sit on a hard-backed chair with your feet hip width apart and your hands resting on your abdominals. Tighten your abdominal muscles as if someone were going to punch you in the stomach. At the same time, press your fingers into your abdomen and contract the muscles tighter in order to resist the pressure of the fingers as much as you can. Hold for 10 seconds, and then relax.

How many? Repeat 5 times.

Top tip
- Keep breathing as you tense the abdominals.

4

5 SIT TO STAND

What for?

This exercise is great for holding correct posture as you stand up and sit down. You should recognize how much work the stomach and leg muscles have to do to in order to maintain correct alignment.

How to do it

a Sit up tall on the edge of a hard-backed chair, with your feet hip width apart and flat on the floor, and your arms relaxed by your sides.

b Stand up, keeping your neck and spine aligned, and without leaning forward or using your arms at all. Then slowly sit yourself back down, but without putting your full weight onto the chair.

How many? Repeat 10 times.

Top tips

- Focus on using your abdominal muscles to help you remain balanced throughout the exercise.
- Keep your arms by your sides, so you are not tempted to support yourself on your thighs.
- When you have mastered this, try the exercise with a book on your head to test your posture.

5a

5b

6 ARM LIFT

What for?

This exercise will work the shoulder blades, open out the chest, and help train your shoulders to sit back and down.

How to do it

a Lie on your front with your arms out to the sides and your elbows bent at right angles. Rest your forehead on the floor, ensuring that your neck stays in line with your spine.

b Lift your arms away from the floor as high as you can, squeezing the shoulder blades together. Hold the position for 5 seconds.

How many? Repeat 10 times.

Top tips

- Move only your arms; keep your torso as still as possible.
- Imagine the shoulder blades sliding together across the back as the arms lift.

6a

6b

7 SIDE LIFT

What for?

This exercise is a real test of integrated core stability—if your body is not perfectly aligned, control and balance will be impossible!

How to do it

a Lie on your left side with your left arm extended and your right arm resting along your side. Make sure your body is in perfect alignment.

b Lift both legs a few inches off the floor and try to hold this balance for 10 seconds. Slowly lower your legs back to the floor.

How many? Repeat 5 times on both sides.

Top tips

• Make sure that your hips are stacked directly on top of each other, and don't roll backward off this position as you lift your legs.

• Keep your core engaged throughout the lift to help maintain balance.

• Imagine that your body is a piece of solid wood, not soggy or bendy in the middle!

• Think of lengthening through your fingers and toes, making yourself as tall as possible throughout the exercise.

7a

7b

8 HAMSTRING STRETCH

What for?

The hamstrings are the muscles that run down the back of your thighs. These can become particularly tight if you sit for long periods of time and are a big factor in bad posture and lower-back pain. This is also a great stretch to do at the end of a long walk.

How to do it

a Lie on your back with your knees bent and your feet flat on the floor. Take hold of your right leg with both hands and, keeping the leg straight and the knee slightly relaxed, ease it in toward your body.

b If you find it hard to reach your leg, use a bathrobe belt or towel to wrap around it.

c If you want to increase the stretch, extend your left leg out along the floor, keeping the right leg extended in the air. Hold the stretch for 30 seconds.

How many? Repeat with the other leg.

Top tips

- Keep the leg you are stretching straight, but avoid locking the knee, as this will put excess pressure on the joint.
- Take a deep breath in, then, as you breathe out, increase the stretch further.
- Avoid over-stretching; work within your own flexibility.
- Keep your head and shoulders relaxed on the floor throughout the exercise.

8a

8b

8c

9 PLANK

What for?

This is a very strong static exercise. It will strengthen the deep abdominal muscles that wrap right around your midsection, giving you a tighter waist and enhanced trunk stability.

How to do it

a Start lying face down on a mat. Place your forearms on the ground with the palms facing down and level with your ears.

b Raise yourself up onto your forearms and the balls of your feet. Keep the shoulders down and back, curl your toes under, and engage your core, making sure that you do not arch your back.

c If you want to increase the intensity of this exercise, raise your knees until your body and legs make a solid straight line—the full plank. Hold the position for 15–30 seconds.

How many? Repeat 2 or 3 times.

Top tips

- Keep your abdominals contracted, and do not allow your back to arch at any point in the exercise.
- Progress to the full plank position only when you can maintain perfect posture in the spine. If you can't, go back to the easier position.
- Keep breathing throughout—it is tempting to hold your breath!
- If you feel any back pain at all, it is better not to do this exercise.

9a

9b

9c

10 BACK EXTENSION

What for?

This exercise is good for strengthening the lower back and is essential for guarding against pain and injury.

How to do it

a Lie on your front with your forehead in contact with the floor and hands resting on your lower back.

b Engage the core and then lift your upper body a few inches away from the floor. Hold for 30 seconds and then, with control, lower yourself back to the floor.

How many? Repeat 10–15 times.

Top tips

- Keep your eyes focused down to the floor throughout the exercise so that the neck stays in line with the rest of the spine.
- Don't try to lift too high off the floor; a few inches is enough.
- To increase the intensity, try placing your hands behind your head.
- If you feel any pain in the lower back, do not continue with the exercise.

10a

Posture "watch-outs"

- Correct yourself if you notice that you are standing with your shoulders slouched forward.
- Never overexaggerate the curve in the lower back.
- Try to avoid carrying something heavy on one side of the body.
- Avoid cradling the telephone between your ear and shoulder.
- Try not to wear high-heeled shoes for long periods of time.
- Always bend your knees and keep your back straight when picking up a heavy object.
- Sleep on a mattress that provides proper back support.
- Sit up straight when watching television instead of slumping in the chair.

10b

YOUR WALKING TECHNIQUE

CHAPTER 3

You may be wondering why on earth you would need to read a chapter on how to walk. After all, you have been doing it quite well without my help since the age of about one or two! However, the key to effective weight-loss is a fast, fat-burning power walk; and for this, technique is all-important—without it you will struggle to increase your pace and your weight-loss results will plateau.

To get the most out of your power walking, your body should work like a finely tuned machine, one movement flowing into the next without any tension or strain. The more comfortable you feel in the movement, the harder you will be able to work, which will of course reap maximum fitness and weight-loss results. Power walking requires many different parts of the body to operate together, and therefore I have broken down the technique so that you can concentrate on arms, legs, feet, torso, etc., in turn before you begin to put it all together. It isn't that the technique is all that difficult, but it will feel different from the way you normally walk and, after years of collecting bad habits, it's a good idea to start from scratch.

Good posture should provide the foundation, as any incorrect alignment requires the body to compensate in order to balance, and this is where it soon starts to feel stiff and injured. It can sometimes be hard to feel what your body is doing, especially when you get your walk up to speed, so ask a friend to watch you as you move and check that each part of the body is doing what it should. It is also a good idea to check your technique at regular intervals after you have started your walking program, just to make sure you haven't slipped back into any bad habits.

Lower body

Setting your stride

The first and most important factor you need to determine about your walk is your stride. So let's have a look at exactly what should be happening each time you take a step.

Finding correct stride length

The most common error that people make when they try to speed up their walk is to take unnaturally big steps. This then throws their posture out of alignment, increasing the risk of injury and wasting a lot of energy into the bargain.

Your stride length is determined by the length of your legs, the flexibility of your hamstrings (muscles in the back of the thighs), and the mobility of your hips. As your joints become more flexible, your hamstrings lengthen, and you lose weight, your stride should lengthen and enable you to increase your speed. However, to begin with, you need to find a stride length that doesn't break the fluidity of your movement. Try this exercise to determine your correct stride.

1

1 Find an area big enough to take about 20 paces forward. Before you start, stand still and check that your posture is in the correct alignment (see page 21). When you are happy that you are standing tall, with relaxed shoulders and an open chest, walk forward at your normal pace and take notice of what happens to your body.

If your head is bobbing up and down and/or you can feel a slight overstretch in the front leg, these are both signs that you are taking too big a stride for your body. Your stride should feel natural and easy, so assess your movement on the basis of its fluidity.

2a

2b

2a & b Now walk again at a normal pace, but this time play around with your stride, making it both longer (a) and shorter (b) until you find the most comfortable position. You should feel that you are walking with ease and maintaining good posture, not overexaggerating the stride.

3 Next, try to increase your speed. Make sure you do this by taking faster steps and not by making your stride longer. Don't try to go too fast at first; just gradually increase the pace as you feel comfortable. You will find, as your strength and stamina increase, and as you get used to the technique, that your speed will feel more natural.

Finding correct stride width

The width of your stride is also an important factor in your walking technique as, if you get it right, you will be able to increase your speed with more ease and waste far less energy. Try the following exercise:

1 Imagine a straight line about the width of a gymnast's beam; or if you want you can use masking tape to mark out a line to practice on. Try walking along the line so that your feet land just on the outside of it. Your feet should slightly overlap one another, but should not be placed directly one in front of the other.

2 Now try putting the stride length, width, and speed all together. It may feel a little odd at first and therefore take a bit more practice until it feels completely natural, but persevere, for in the long run it will save you endless time and energy and help to protect you from injury.

1

2

Swing those hips

You will notice as you change your stride that your hips will swing from side to side slightly more than usual.

This is a movement that happens naturally once you adjust your stride width and length, and the pelvis and hip area move freely so that the legs can stride out. However, take care not to exaggerate the movement. It shouldn't be as pronounced as that of the race walkers you see on television, and should just facilitate fluidity.

Feet and legs

Before a walk, at the same time as you check your posture for correct alignment, give each leg a gentle shake to make sure that the leg and knee muscles are relaxed and not too stiff. Remember to do this regularly as it is important not to lock the knee joint either when the heel strikes the ground or when the toes push off, as this can exert an awkward strain and lead to stiffness and pain.

The feet are of key importance in walking, as when you stride, one foot always remains in contact with the ground. The heel should strike the ground first, and the toes should provide a dynamic push-off to launch you into the next step. Follow this step-by-step heel-toe action:

1 Start by taking a step forward with your right leg. The front heel should hit the floor first with the ankle flexed at an angle of about 45 degrees.

2 You should then roll through the length of the foot as you transfer the weight forward, being careful not to slap the foot down.

3 Then push off through the ball and toes just as the other foot is in complete contact with the ground and bring the back leg forward to strike again with the heel, making sure that the foot isn't dragged along the ground or lifted too high—an inch or two of clearance is about right.

1

2

3

Measuring your stride

It is really important for your walking program that you know the average length of your stride, because this information allows you to calculate how fast and how far you are walking and to set yourself targets to work towards. If you have a pedometer, it should be able to calculate all the above, and may even be able to tell you how many calories you've burned.

If you don't have a pedometer you can still estimate the distance you travel by measuring your stride, then counting the number of steps you take in 1 minute; if you multiply this number by your stride length, it will give you the distance traveled in 1 minute.

To measure your stride, you will need a friend to help you, and a tape measure. Find a space where you have room to walk at least 20 steps. Start walking, trying to get into your natural rhythm and speed and, when you have reached your average walking pace, stop mid-stride at the point where your feet are farthest apart.

Ask your friend to measure the distance between the heel of your front foot and the toes of your back foot. This will be your stride length. Then repeat the exercise a few times so that you can record the average distance.

Upper body

Head

Your head should be in a neutral position when you walk, looking neither up nor down. A good way of checking this is to make sure your chin is parallel to the ground.

When you start walking, focus on something about 16–20 feet (5–6 metres) in front of you. Although you will need to look down from time to time to see where you are walking, you should try to avoid moving with the neck as much as possible.

Shoulders

Your shoulders should stay relaxed and down throughout the walk as it won't help your arm swing if your shoulders are tense or hunched over. Think about your correct posture setup: keep your chest open and head level, stay relaxed, and then the shoulders should naturally avoid too much tension.

Torso

To maintain correct posture when walking, you will need to use your midsection, which means keeping your abdominal muscles active to support your lower back. Pull your navel in toward your spine and grow tall through the crown of your head as this will keep your spine supported and lengthened throughout your walk. Tuck your pelvis in so that the lower back remains strong and aligned and the hips move freely to create a fluid stride.

Arms

Using the correct arm technique is crucial to a successful power walk, as they help to propel you forward and increase your speed just as much as the legs do.

With the right movement, they also allow you to increase the intensity of your workout without walking faster or for any longer. The controlled but forceful arm-and-shoulder swing works the upper body extremely hard and improves muscle strength as well as causing the heart to beat faster.

If you are not used to power walking, the arms may ache a bit at first and you may also feel a little self-conscious striding around the place. However, it is worth persevering, since the right arm action will allow you to move more rhythmically and far more efficiently in the long run.

1

2

1 Start with your arms bent at a 90-degree angle, and hold this position throughout your walk. As you start walking, swing your arms in opposition, keeping them close in toward your body. The movement should come from the shoulders, and you should almost feel the arms brushing past your hips each time they swing.

Make sure that you are not exaggerating the arms. Your hand should reach no higher than chin height when coming forward and no farther than the hip when going back.

2 Check the shape of your hands. They should not be clenched into a tight fist but just loosely cupped, as if you were holding something delicate between your thumb and fingers.

Breathing control

Oxygen is vital to us and we can't survive for longer than a few minutes without it. The problem is that, even though we all breathe and take in oxygen, very few of us breathe deeply enough. We take shallow breaths, directing air into our chest area rather than making use of the full capacity of our lungs, and the muscles that expand the lungs lie largely out of use.

Walking is aerobic exercise, which means "with oxygen." When you walk, oxygen is delivered to the internal organs and working muscles via the bloodstream and is then used to burn fat for energy. As you step up the intensity of your walk you increase the workload and will need to breathe more deeply to provide your body with the extra oxygen that it requires. If you are not breathing correctly, you are likely to get very out of breath.

To breathe correctly means breathing deeply using the diaphragm, the muscle that sits below the chest area and moves up and down as you breathe in and out, making room for the lungs to expand and then helping to squeeze the air back out.

At rest, most people fill their lungs with about 14 fluid ounces (0.4 liters) of air. However, the lungs have the capacity to take in ten times that amount. By practicing deep belly breathing during exercise, you can train them to take in more air, even when at rest, and, as your fitness level improves, to make it possible for the body to use the oxygen far more efficiently.

Abdominal breathing exercise

1 Lie on your back with your hands resting on your abdomen. Make sure your neck is in line with the rest of the spine and your shoulders are relaxed and down. Breathe normally and take note of what your body is doing. See if your chest is rising and falling as you breathe in and out.

2 Now try to direct the breath into the abdominal area. Think about using the diaphragm to draw the breath in and out of the body. You should notice that your hands are rising and falling with your abdomen as you breathe in and out. There should be very little, if any, movement in the chest area.

Stay here for a while until abdominal breathing feels more comfortable. You should notice how you can breathe much more deeply.

You should be breathing in this way all the time, so try to become aware of your techniqe as you go about everyday chores, and correct yourself if necessary—the more you practice, the more this will become second nature. Deep abdominal breathing is also a great stress releaser, so at those manic times in the day, just take a few moments to breathe properly.

1

2

The complete technique

Now it is time to put all the separate elements of this technique together. Don't worry if you find it hard to coordinate your arms, legs, feet, and breathing the first time! It will take a little getting used to.

1 Start by standing tall, with your feet slightly apart and arms by your sides—take a moment to check your postural alignment. Make sure you are engaging your core by pulling your navel in toward your spine; check that you are focusing 16–20 feet (5–6 metres) in front of you so your chin is level; check that your shoulders are relaxed and down, and that you are lengthening tall through the crown of your head. Concentrate on breathing into the abdominals.

2 Bring your arms into position ready for your walk, checking that your elbows are bent at a 90-degree angle and that your hands are lightly cupped rather than clenched into a fist.

3 Start to walk by taking a step forward with your right foot; remembering to lead with the heel. Use your arms in opposition, so your left arm moves forward as your right arm moves back. As your heel makes contact with the floor, start to transfer your weight onto the right foot.

4 Keep transferring your weight, passing through a position where your weight is evenly distributed between both feet. Your left arm should be still moving forward and your right arm back.

5 Keep transferring your weight onto your right foot; the left foot should be up on the ball to propel you forward. As the weight moves fully onto the right leg, your left leg should extend behind. The arms should be in maximum position: the front hand no higher than chin height and the back hand no lower than the hip.

6 Your left leg should then bend, passing through the middle, ready to step again. Start bringing your left arm back and your right arm forward ready to swing through the center before coming forwards.

7 Now you are ready to start again, this time bringing the left leg forward, leading with the heel, and beginning to swing the right arm forward and the left arm back.

Mistakes to watch out for

Forward posture

Leaning forward when you walk is often associated with bad posture and looking down. However, if you think about your posture setup before you start walking your breathing will feel far easier and give you a better workout. Think about keeping your focus on a point 16–20 feet (5–6 metres) ahead to avoid looking at the ground in front of you.

Straight arms

When you are concentrating on walking fast, it is common to forget about the swing and walk with straight, rigid arms. However, it is much harder to walk at any speed without the propelling motion of the arms and it can also lead to swollen, tingling or numb fingers owing to increased blood flow to the fingertips.

Forgetting to breathe

It is very easy, once you start concentrating on the movement, to forget about breathing! Some people find they hold their breath for a few steps at a time. Try to think about getting into a pattern, counting the number of steps to each in and out breath and making it the same each time.

Side-to-side arms

Another common mistake is to allow the arms to swing from side to side rather than forward and backward. Even though the arms are bent at right angles, you can find that the front arm crosses the line of the body and the back arm falls out to the side.

Common Injuries

Although taking the right precautions can substantially reduce the chances of injury, it is still quite likely that most of us will deal with some kind of muscle strain or other common injury in our life. It is important, therefore, that we learn to recognize the signs of injury and take the appropriate course of action to avoid making it worse (see box opposite).

If you experience any symptoms such as tenderness, swelling, bruising, or pain when moving, you should stop walking. With less serious strains and pulls, a few days' rest often sets you on the road to recovery but if you are experiencing a lot of discomfort, you may want to see a doctor.

Shin splints

This is the walker's most common injury—an acute pain, throbbing, or tenderness down the front of the shin, which is often accompanied by inflammation. Beginners are particularly susceptible as walking gives the shin muscles a vigorous workout as they contract and extend to flex and point the foot, and overdoing it can make them feel very tender.

Shin splints can also be attributed to an imbalance between strong, tight calf muscles and weak shin muscles, often the result of wearing high heels, and to walking or jogging on a hard surface such as concrete.

Try where possible to walk on a soft surface such as grass, and check the fit of your shoes for wearing too-large running shoes can make your toes grip automatically as you walk, awkwardly clenching the shins.

For treatment, ice the area for 10–15 minutes, 3 times a day, to reduce swelling. Make sure you take a rest from power walking for at least 2 or 3 days, and when you restart your program, begin slowly and gradually build back up to your current schedule.

Sprains

A sprain is an injury to a ligament that supports a joint and is usually the result of a twist or tumble. Symptoms of a sprain can include swelling, bruising, and general weakness and applying pressure to the injured area is often painful.

To treat a sprain you should apply an ice pack for 10–15 minutes, 3 times a day. Elevate the area as much as possible, and rest until it has completely healed. When you restart your walking program, build up gradually to strengthen the area again; if you know that you have weak ankles, protect the area with a support bandage.

Muscle strains

When you strain or pull a muscle, it means that there has been some damage to the muscle or its attaching tendons. Injuries vary in severity—a light strain will result in a little weakness to the area, but sometimes it means that the muscle fibers have been torn, leading to the small blood vessels being damaged, which may cause local bleeding and bruising. With the latter, you will experience swelling, redness, and an inability to use the muscle.

Apply ice to the area as soon as possible, and keep it elevated. You can take aspirin and ibuprofen to take down the swelling and reduce the pain and to improve your ability to move around. It's also advisable to rest until the swelling and pain have gone, and gradually build back into your program, giving the injured area a chance to regain strength and flexibility.

Muscle cramps

When you have been for a long walk, it is not uncommon to experience cramp, a painful muscle spasm in your feet, calves, or thighs shortly after you have finished. This is due to a buildup of lactic acid in the muscles or a lack of sodium as a result of heavy sweating. It should last only a few minutes, and the best thing to do to relieve it is to stretch the muscle out and massage it gently until the pain goes away.

Stitches

A stitch is best described as a sharp pain under the rib cage that usually accompanies shortness of breath. This is because it is cramp of a kind, located in the diaphragm, that can be brought on by pushing yourself too hard, or by eating just before your workout. The best way of getting rid of it is to change your breathing pattern for a minute—holding your breath often helps.

The RICE formula for injuries

Rest the injured area. Avoid the activity that caused the injury and other activities that are painful.

Ice the area to relieve pain and help the swelling go down.

Compression can be gently applied with an elastic bandage or strapping, providing support and reducing swelling. Make sure you don't wrap it too tightly or you will cut off the blood supply to the area.

Elevate the injured area to decrease swelling. Use a chair to prop up an injured leg or a sling bandage to raise your arm.

WHICH WAY TO WALK

While power walking will probably be the most beneficial and convenient type of exercise for you to incorporate into your weight-loss program, other walking styles have their plus points, too. Hill walking, for example, is great for burning fat while also building lower-body strength and toning up those thighs. Together with hiking, it allows you to escape your regular routine and enjoy the simple pleasures of space, freedom, and fresh air outdoors. Nordic walking is excellent exercise for weight-loss, as the poles provide the upper body with a thorough workout and really take the intensity up a notch. Walking clubs are invaluable for giving you peer-group support, which is motivation in itself, and race and charity walks provide clear-sighted goals to train towards and can also be extremely enjoyable events.

Once you've reached a good level of fitness, try out these different styles to see which you enjoy and which will allow you to take your walking further. All bring great cardiovascular benefits, and by mixing different walking techniques you will keep your program varied and interesting. For example, combining the different terrains of road walking and hill walking presents a more rounded challenge for the body and guards against repetitive strains.

Walking is a fantastic form of exercise which everyone can enjoy, regardless of their age, as all you have to do is adapt the pace and environment to your level of fitness. There are so many ways you can vary your walks that I will be touching on only a few here. However, feel free to explore further!

Nordic walking

Also called skiwalking, Nordic walking is fast catching on as a serious fitness craze—it originated in Finland as a summer training method for cross-country skiers and was then developed into a fitness exercise with specific training equipment in co-operation with the Finnish sports equipment manufacturer Excel Oyj, researchers in sports medicine, and other fitness professionals.

The key to Nordic walking is the way it combines power walking with weight-bearing, ski-like poles, which can raise the intensity of your workout by as much as 20 percent. Whereas carrying ordinary weights can put a strain on your posture and slow down your speed, the poles are lightweight and make it possible for you to work your upper and lower body while power walking, rather than just the legs.

It is estimated that Europe already has 3.5 million committed Nordic walkers—most of them in Europe, although more and more Americans are taking up this activity. Nordic walking is widely endorsed by politicians and businesses. Its ability to boost fitness levels is well documented, and in Germany the government refunds the cost of attending a certified course for hospital outpatients, while two health insurance firms in Switzerland reward policy holders with financial bonuses if they attend Nordic walking courses.

Nordic walking poles are flexible and specifically designed so that you use your arms to push off with them to propel yourself forward as you walk and then create extra resistance as you push against them when planting them into the ground. The complete range of movement means that the upper body is called upon to do significantly more work than in other walking styles. Indeed, enthusiasts say it uses 90 percent of the body's skeletal muscles, compared to, say, swimming, which uses 35 percent, or running which uses 70 percent. Increased muscle use translates as more energy expended and really maximizes the calorie-burning potential of a simple activity such as walking (the average Nordic walker burns off up to 46 per cent more calories than a regular walker).

However, even though you are using more muscle groups and expending more energy, Nordic walking can actually feel easier than many other type of vigorous exercise, because the effort is spread more evenly throughout the body. The intensity you walk at is determined by your upper-body effort, and therefore you can walk in groups of varying fitness abilities and still work out at your optimal level. Nordic walking is a very sociable activity, and by sharing fitness goals, you are far more likely to stick to your weight-loss program, and you get the fresh-air benefits of being outside as well.

Another benefit of Nordic walking is that the spine rotates as the poles swing in opposition to your stride and this increases the mobility and strength of the spinal disks. The movement utilizes the large muscles of the back, which pull down the shoulder blades, significantly reducing neck and shoulder tension and guarding against the onset of back pain. And because the arms take more of the

strain, a lighter load is placed on the knees and other lower body joints, allowing people of all ages to exercise with more comfort than during normal walking or jogging.

Even when you are exercising extremely hard and placing a lot of weight on the arms, your rate of perceived exertion (RPE) during Nordic walking is often quite low, and it is surprising to find out just how hard your heart is working, while you are feeling relatively comfortable. Wear a heart-rate monitor when out walking and I guarantee you will be pleasantly surprised.

Nordic walking should be practiced for relatively long periods—that is, between half an hour and two hours at a time. The pace should be steady, and the heart rate should rise to between 120 and 150 beats per minute (see how to measure your exercise intensity on page 93, as this will be dependent on your age and ability). However, because of the customary high heart-rate response and low RPE, you can often Nordic walk at a higher intensity, for longer, and with more ease than in many other types of training and achieve your fitness target with little stress and less sweat.

Benefits at a glance

• Heart rate is 5–17 beats per minute higher (for example, in normal walking heart rate is 130 beats/minute and in Nordic walking 147 beats/minute: i.e., increase is 13 percent)
• Energy consumption increases when using poles by an average of 20 percent compared with ordinary walking without poles
• Releases pain and muscle tension in the neck and shoulders
• Reduces the load on knees and other joints

Choosing poles

If you're going to give Nordic walking a try, the first thing you need to do is get yourself some poles. When buying poles, look for the following:

• grip comfort—well-padded wrist straps for long walks
• interchangeable grip system – guarantees flexibility and comfort
• light weight—so they can swing comfortably
• changeable angled spike tip—many have hard metal tips, which are good for stability on natural terrain, and removable rubber covers for walking on roads and sidewalks
• adjustable height—makes them easier to store and share. Before you begin walking, always adjust your poles to the correct length (see box below)
• good shock absorption—a high carbon content in the glass fiber/carbon blend results in better shock absorption and therefore greater comfort

Find the right pole height

Nordic walking poles should be about 70 percent of your body height. They are quite tall, but this is to ensure maximum forward thrust. To calculate the correct pole height for you, follow this simple formula: your height in inches (or centimeters) x 0.68.

Pole lengths are graded in 2 in (5 cm) intervals, so round up to the nearest 5cm. The rule of thumb is that when you hold the grip with the tip on the ground, your elbow should be at an angle of approximately 90 degrees.

Correct pole technique

With Nordic walking poles, the exertion of the arm movement is channeled to the pole tip by means of a properly adjusted wrist strap, rather than by a tight hand grip on the poles themselves, as this allows the poles to swing and ensures a fluid, flexible type of stride and motion when walking.

1 Place your hands in the straps, which look a bit like fingerless gloves and are usually attached to the pole with a trigger release mechanism. Hold the pole at the base of the thumb and base of the index finger, and rest the remaining fingers lightly on the grip.

2 When holding the poles, lean very slightly forward with your shoulders down and look up and straight in front of you. Keep the poles close to the body, pointing diagonally backward at all times.

3 The hand should grip the pole every time it is planted in the ground and then let go as the pole is drawn back behind the body, finishing with an open hand. The strap will keep the pole in position as you release your hold.

4 With each forward step, place the pole in the ground to the side of you, so that you then walk past it and the pole arm extends and straightens. The rule of thumb is that with Nordic walking, the poles spend most of the time behind you and diagonally pointing back.

5 Do not forget to plant the pole into the ground at every step, for merely swinging the poles back and forth will not benefit your workout as much as planting your pole and levering off it with every step.

Putting it all together

With good Nordic walking technique you are aiming to increase the work of the upper body, slightly exaggerating your normal walking movement but without compromising on your natural rhythm.

1 Start with a posture check—look up, engage the core, breathe with the diaphragm, and open out your chest. Relax your shoulders and, with your arms hanging loosely by your sides, keep your hands open and allow the straps to hold the poles.

2 Start to walk forward with a fluid stride, checking that you have the correct foot technique, which will give your calf muscles a good workout. The heel should hit the ground first, before you roll through to the ball of the foot and push off with the toes as you propel yourself forward into the next step.

3 Once you feel comfortable with your stride, start to swing your arms from the shoulders (elbows bent at a right angle), keeping them quite close to the body for a compact and streamlined movement. Each time you take a step, the opposite arm should swing forward to waist height, no higher. Keep your hands open at this point so that the poles are held by the straps and concentrate instead on arm and leg coordination.

4 When you are happy with this, take hold of the poles lightly in your hand. On the forward arm swing, gently grip the pole and plant it into the ground a little behind the heel of the advancing foot.

5 As you walk forward and your body passes the pole, you need to push off with the trailing arm. As the pole is drawn back behind the body, you should release the grip and open the hand. This creates a greater stretch in your arm and greater spinal rotation.

6 With a little practice you should soon be able to coordinate the legs, arms, and poles so that the movement feels fluid and natural. There should be a clear swing of the hips and shoulders, and they should be in a counter-swinging motion with the lower body—it's a common mistake for beginners to combine a right arm and a right leg, but it should always be a pair of opposites: right leg, left arm.

7 When walking uphill, you use the same basic technique as for flat terrain, but lean forward into the gradient as you would for hill walking—the leverage you get from the poles is great for powering you up to the top.

Walking downhill is a little different, as you should keep the poles behind you, rather than planting them in front, so that they can provide support if you lose your footing. This is great for stability and really means you can control your descent. As in regular walking, it is also a good idea to bend your knees so that you lower your center of gravity, especially on steep slopes.

Exercise for everyone

One of the great strengths of Nordic Walking is its accessibility, for people of all ages and fitness levels can do it comfortably and safely. The poles provide great stability for those who are no longer quite so steady on their feet, and there are even techniques that can adapt to arthiritis in the hands and upper arms. Ex-runners love its high intensity and low impact, which mean they can maintain their fitness levels, and anyone who has been relatively inactive for a while can take it up with confidence.

Mall walking

Mall walking, or "mallercise" as it is sometimes called, was born in the United States fifty years ago, when the first-ever completely undercover shopping center was opened in Minnesota. Local doctors began to advise their cardiac patients to exercise there as part of their recovery program; and it has since become so popular that there are now believed to be over 1 million people mall walking across the country.

Mall walking has recently started to spread throughout the rest of the world as health professionals and exercisers alike are realizing the benefits of having an indoor walking venue, especially during the winter months. Some shopping centers are even offering special membership programs, in which members receive incentives such as early opening times, store discounts, educational speakers, and special maps of the mall that make it easy to track your distance on each level.

Regardless of whether there is a specially set up mall-walking group or membership program in your area, this really is a fantastic way to keep walking. Most shopping centers are open seven days a week, you can go early or late to avoid the crowds, and you don't need to worry about what the weather is doing outside, so can avoid the pitfalls of wind, rain, snow, and intense heat. At the same time, you won't have to breathe in noxious traffic fumes or worry about crossing streets; and if you are walking alone, you can be assured of your personal safety, since there are people around, stores open, and security guards on duty.

The downside to mall walking is that it can become a little tedious walking around and around a lap that even in the largest of centers is at best 1 mile (1.6 kilometers) long, although there is always the benefit of window shopping at the same time! Another drawback is that the floors are mostly concrete, and repetitive walking on a hard surface will take its toll on your shins. Make absolutely sure that your footwear provides good cushioning to absorb the shock, and replace your shoes before they wear out to avoid injury.

When mall walking, it is important to set yourself goals; otherwise you could find yourself walking around in circles with no real purpose. Before you start, find out the distance of each circuit and set yourself both a target number of laps to complete in each session and a target distance to build up to. Gradually increase your distance each time you walk, and when you have achieved your target, try to improve on your time. Keep setting yourself new goals as you progress.

If you would like to be part of a mall-walking group but can't find one in your local area, consider setting up your own. Talk to your local government; they may be receptive to ideas for new health initiatives.

Hill walking

CHAPTER 4

Walking up hills or through hilly terrain can be a thoroughly stimulating and fulfilling experience. It's wonderful to be out in the countryside, breathing in the fresh air, but there are serious fitness benefits to be enjoyed, too!

Adding a gradient to your walking route significantly increases your workload and calorie expenditure; and, believe it or not, even walking back down the hill uses more energy than if you were walking on flat ground, and it really works those legs. If you don't believe me, try wearing a heart rate monitor next time you tackle a hill—I guarantee you will be amazed at just how quickly your heart rate responds to the challenge!

Moving your body weight up a gradient dramatically increases the load on your muscles and requires you to put in much more effort. On really steep inclines, it's not unusual for even a fit person's heart rate to increase by about 20 percent, and going downhill you really have to contract your leg muscles to work against gravity and slow down your descent.

Hill walking requires a slightly different technique, simply to work with the terrain. Lean forward into the slope to keep your balance, and take slightly shorter stride lengths as you climb uphill, because this makes the quadriceps, the large muscles of your thighs, do most of the hard work.

Going down steep slopes can be a strain on fragile knees and hip joints. Take smaller steps and don't lean backward. Bend the knees slightly so that they don't lock and become stiff, and if the gradient is especially steep, weave down in hairpin bends, which should prevent you from skidding.

Nature was great at giving us hills for all levels of ability, so you can choose the difficulty level of your walk by the size and distance of your hill. Start small, gradually building your fitness, navigation skills, and confidence.

There really isn't anything more satisfying than reaching the top of a big hill and seeing how far you have come—and enjoying the magnificent view!

Hiking

Hiking is countryside walking that is often done as part of a group. These groups may follow a set route using bridlepaths, marked paths, national trails, national parks, and common land. You will be able to find out about your appropriate group by looking in the phone book; or if you want to walk alone, you can find out about routes by contacting the local government department of tourism.

The real appeal of rambling is getting out in the fresh air in beautiful surroundings and walking a route through varying terrain that you can tailor to your level of fitness. Joining a hiking club has some great benefits, too. You will find it much easier to motivate yourself, first to go out for your walk, and secondly to walk for longer and farther with the encouragement of others. There are also great social benefits, as you will make new friends and share experiences with other members of the club.

Safety on rural walks

Whether you are walking alone or with a group, you should plan your route before you set out, take a map and compass, and make sure you know how to use them. These skills are very easily learned from a friend or member of the group.

• Make sure you are wearing the appropriate clothing for your walk (see page 114).

• Check the weather forecast before you set out. The higher the hill you are climbing, the more unpredictable the weather may be, so be prepared with all-weather clothing (see page 114).

• It's an easy mistake to underestimate the amount of time you may be out when hill walking, which may mean you get caught out on the hill after dark. Remember that you move at a much slower speed when walking uphill than when you are on level ground. Always estimate beforehand how long you think a walk should take and allow plenty of time.

• If walking in a group, always plan your route according to the ability of the weakest member.

• Always take your cellphone with you when you are walking in remote areas. In the event of an emergency it will save valuable time if you are able to contact the emergency services immediately, although cellphone network signals can be nonexistent in some rural areas. If so, you may have to make your way to a public telephone.

Do you know the Country Code?

If you are going to be walking through countryside or woodland, you should follow the "Leave No Trace" code of outdoor ethics. This consists of seven basic principles, details of which can be obtained from www.lnt.org. The basic principles are:

• Plan ahead and prepare.
• Travel and camp on durable surfaces.
• Dispose of waste properly.
• Leave what you find.
• Minimize campfire impacts.
• Respect wildlife.
• Be considerate of other visitors.

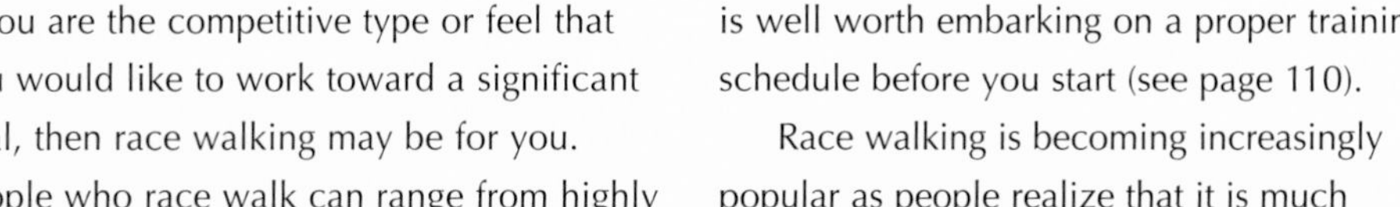

Race walking

If you are the competitive type or feel that you would like to work toward a significant goal, then race walking may be for you. People who race walk can range from highly trained athletes to charity walkers, often found holding their own in the middle of the local fundraising fun run.

Although racing should be enjoyable, a good race does take thorough planning, and it is well worth embarking on a proper training schedule before you start (see page 110).

Race walking is becoming increasingly popular as people realize that it is much gentler on your joints than high-impact running and yet is every bit as challenging and technically demanding as running a marathon.

The big difference between race walking and running is that the competitor has to remain in contact with the ground at all times, and as the front leg hits the ground it should be straight and remain straight until the knee passes under the body. Judges can give fouls and disqualify the race walker if they feel that their technique is incorrect.

If you are interested in race walking, you should find out if there is a local club and what races you could train for locally. It might be best to start with a fun/charity race and work your way up. Who knows—maybe you will walk the marathon!

Walking vacations

Walking vacations are a great way to keep fit and unwind and also give you the opportunity to see parts of the world on a much more personal level than if you were on a package deal or sightseeing in your car.

There is so much choice these days; you can walk in almost every country of the world, for short or long breaks, alone or in a group, with or without a guide, etc.—the list is endless. You could choose a gentle walking environment or set yourself a challenge with ambitious walking terrain such as in the Rockies or the Himalayas. Whatever you decide to do, check beforehand how fit you need to be for each itinerary, so that you can select a holiday that suits your level of ability. Decide whether you want to be based in one place or move on each night, and whether you want to carry all your luggage on your back or have porters to take the load.

If you think about all the details before you go, you won't be in for any unpleasant surprises, and you'll find that there is truly no more inspiring or exhilarating way to experience the most captivating places in the world. You will almost certainly return home with a real sense of achievement.

Charity walks

If you like the idea of having a reason to get walking but are not sure you are ready for race walking, why not try a charity walk? This is less competitive and the aim is to complete a set course, or your own goal, rather than walk at speed. You can walk at your own pace around the course and even walk with family and friends.

The real bonus of charity walks is that while you are getting fit you are also helping to raise money for a deserving charity. You usually find you pay an entrance fee for the race, or that the fee will be waived if you collect a minimum amount of sponsorship.

If there is a particular charity that you would like to raise some money for, why not contact it and find out if there is an event planned in your local area.

Treadmills

Unfortunately, treadmills don't allow you to enjoy the benefits of the great outdoors, but on days when the weather is really bad, they provide the ideal solution.

In fact, treadmills are very useful pieces of equipment, as most are designed with preset programs that allow you to follow a cardiovascular or fat-burning workout that simulates all different kinds of terrain. Many will also calculate your heart rate, speed, and pace and even count how many calories you have burned, and you can constantly keep an eye on your intensity levels by looking down at the control panel in front of you.

Treadmills are sprung and are therefore much softer and easier to walk on than a hard road, and place less strain on your joints. However, this also means that, on a flat setting, the treadmill doesn't require the same level of exertion from you as outdoor terrain. Therefore, it is a good idea to set it on a slight incline to ensure that you are walking at the same intensity as you would outdoors.

When using a treadmill, the trick is to start off slowly and increase your speed gradually. Let go of the handrails only when you feel confident, and then don't forget to pump your arms (most gym equipment is positioned in front of full-length mirrors, so take the opportunity to check your posture and technique). When you are ready to get off the machine, reduce the speed slowly and take a minute for your body to adapt to a nonmoving floor—if you walk away too quickly your legs may feel a little wobbly!

WARMING UP AND

COOLING DOWN

CHAPTER 5

Warming up and cooling down are integral to any exercise program and yet I often see people in the gym who skip these most crucial parts of their workout. This always fills me with horror, as I wonder if they realize what a risk it can be.

Warming up prepares the body for the activity that is to come. As soon as you start gentle exercise, changes begin to take place in the body. Your respiratory rate increases, the blood flows faster through the body, and your body temperature rises. With this, hormones are released; both these dilate the blood vessels, enabling more blood to be diverted to the working muscles, and strengthen the heartbeat, so that more oxygen-rich blood is pumped to every organ. The body is primed for a higher level of exertion and therefore knows what to expect. In many ways, it is no different from a car which is understandably a little temperamental when cold and which you wouldn't dream of driving at 100 mph (160 kph) until it had had a chance to warm up. In fact, you would probably be in danger of damaging the engine even attempting to do so!

Warming up also takes care of the body by significantly reducing the risk of injury. During gentle activity, synovial fluid is released; this lubricates the joints and makes muscles more supple and elastic. Think of a piece of poster putty, which is much more likely to snap if pulled apart when cold rather than when warm and pliable; the body acts in the same way.

Use your warm-up as an opportunity to find your concentration. We all try to fit in exercise around our busy schedules, and therefore it is a good idea to take a few minutes to focus on what you are doing and what you want to get out of it. There is no need to rush, and this way you are much more likely to enjoy the workout and to achieve the goals you have set.

What should I include in my warm-up?

The first aim in your warm-up is to increase your body temperature slowly, as this gives your muscles and tendons time to prepare themselves for the demands you will make on them during the workout to come. You can do this in a variety of ways. If you were in the gym, you would probably go for a piece of cardiovascular equipment, such as the stepper, bike, treadmill, or rower. However, this generally isn't an option at home and so the best way to get warm is to walk at a gentle pace—certainly nowhere near the intensity you are looking to achieve during the main body of your workout.

The second stage should incorporate some stretches to improve motion around the joints and to protect against injury. It is very important that you stretch only after you have taken the time to get the body moving, as mucles can only achieve maximum performance when all their blood vessels are dilated and once the increased blood flow has enabled greater flexibility. At rest, muscles only use 15–20 percent of blood flow, compared to 70 percent, or more, after only 10 minutes of activity.

Once you have finished your stretches, you should then gradually raise your heart rate until you have reached the impact level you want to sustain for the main workout. On page 69 I have laid out a warm-up routine that will prepare you specifically for the *Walking for Weight-Loss* program.

What should I include in my cool-down?

Cooling down is the exact opposite of warming up, and it is just as essential. In slowing to a much gentler pace, the aim is gradually to return your heart rate, respiration rate, and body temperature to normal and provide a safe and effective recovery from physical activity.

It is very important that you do not stop cardiovascular activity suddenly without a winding-down process. As you exercise, blood is pumped around the body quickly; this is aided by the muscles in the leg, particularly the calf muscles, which contract as you walk and help to push the blood up the leg and around the body. If you suddenly stop walking, the muscles stop working, causing blood to pool in the legs. This means that there is also insufficient blood flow to the brain, which can make you feel light-headed and dizzy, and potentially lead to varicose veins.

The second stage of the cool-down process is to stretch out all the major muscle groups and to hold the stretch for longer than in your warm-up in order to increase your flexibility. If you stretch regularly, you will be amazed how supple you become, which will be of real benefit as the years go by. Also, if you relax into your stretches you will find that they become a genuine pleasure rather than a chore and provide a good opportunity to reflect on your workout and what you have achieved.

Your warm-up

CHAPTER 5

Make sure you have enough layers on to keep you warm while your body temperature is still low. You can take these off as you get warmer, but replace them again if you get cold at any point. Perform the following exercises in order, taking particular care that you keep warm in between any static stretches.

1

1 GENTLE WALKING

What for?

To raise your heart rate, respiration rate, and body temperature gradually, slowly preparing your body for the more vigorous exercise to come.

How to do it

Start walking at a steady but gentle pace for 5–10 minutes, gradually raising your body temperature until you feel warm.

Top tips

- Don't walk so fast that you feel out of breath.
- If it is particularly cold outside, you may need to walk for longer to feel warm.
- At this stage, don't push your body to do anything it isn't ready for.

2 NECK STRETCH

What for?

To stretch, mobilize, and release any tension from the neck. The muscles in the neck are particularly sensitive to pulls and cricks when they are cold, so this is a great exercise to make sure the muscles are thoroughly warm before you start.

How to do it

a Stand with your feet hip width apart and the knees slightly relaxed. Take your left arm over your head and place the hand on your right ear or as close as your flexibility will allow.

b Using your hand to apply gentle pressure, tilt your head to the left side, lowering the ear

2a

2b

toward the shoulder as far as feels comfortable. Hold the stretch for 10 seconds, and then slowly bring your head back to the center.

How many? Perform the stretch once on each side.

Top tips

• Keep your nose and eyes pointing forward all the way through the stretch.

• Don't pull on the head; just allow the weight of the hand to apply gentle pressure as the head tilts.

• Take your time to tilt the head to avoid pulling a muscle.

3 SHOULDER CIRCLE

What for?

To mobilize the shoulders and upper back in preparation for your walking arm technique.

How to do it

Stand with your feet hip width apart and your knees slightly relaxed, arms hanging loosely by your sides.

Lift your elbows slightly out to the sides and start to circle your shoulders back, making the movement progressively bigger and bigger.

How many? Circle 15–20 times and then repeat, circling the shoulders forward.

Top tips

• Make sure the movement is controlled.

• Try to keep the shoulders relaxed throughout the movement.

3

4 TRICEPS STRETCH

What for?
To stretch the triceps muscle (in the back of each upper arm) which will work hard once you start your power walk.

How to do it
a Stand with your feet hip width apart and your knees slightly relaxed, arms by your sides. Extend your right arm up above your head, keeping it close to your ear.

b Drop your right forearm as far down your back as your flexibility will allow, then lift your left arm and use the left hand to push back on your elbow, gently increasing the stretch. Hold for 10 seconds.

How many? Perform the stretch once with each arm.

Top tips
- Use your left hand to keep the elbow pulled in toward the ear, at the same time pushing back on the elbow to increase the stretch.
- Make sure you keep your core engaged to avoid arching your back as you reach the arm down the spine.
- Apply gentle pressure on the elbow—you should feel the stretch, but it shouldn't be uncomfortable.

4a

4b

5 BACK AND HAMSTRING STRETCH

What for?
To mobilize the spine and stretch the muscles down the back of your upper legs in preparation for your power walk.

How to do it
a Stand with your feet hip width apart and your knees slightly relaxed, arms down by your sides, looking straight ahead. Slowly, leading with your head, start to roll down through the spine, allowing your arms to relax toward the floor.

b Roll down as far as your flexibility will allow, placing your hands on the floor if possible. Hold the position for 10 seconds, and then slowly reverse the motion by rolling back up through the spine and bringing the head up last.

How many? Repeat 3–4 times.

Top tips
• Don't allow your knees to lock as you progress through the movement. Keep them straight, if possible, to maximize the hamstring stretch, but slightly relaxed.
• Think about working through each vertebra, one at a time, as you roll down, and think about stacking them back one on top of the other as you roll up to standing.
• Keep the movement under control all the way through.

5a

5b

6 HIP FLEXOR STRETCH

What for?

To prepare and stretch the hip flexors (muscles that bend a part of the body) for the pendulum motion of the legs when power walking.

How to do it

Stand with your feet together and your arms by your sides. Step your left leg back so that your right knee bends, and keep sliding the foot back until you are in a full lunge position with your right knee directly aligned over the right ankle. Place both hands on your right thigh for support.

Holding the position, ease your hips forward slightly until you can feel the stretch increase down the front of your hips. Hold this position for 10 seconds, then slowly bring your left foot back to standing.

How many? Perform the stretch once with each leg.

Top tips

- In the lunge position make sure your front knee is directly over the ankle so that your shinbone is an upright vertical, not at an angle. This will ensure that you do not put undue pressure on the knees.
- Keeping your body upright will ensure that you feel the stretch in the hips.

6

7 LEG SWING

What for?

This is a great exercise to loosen up the hips and get the legs moving in preparation for your walking.

How to do it

a Stand sideways on to a tree or lamppost, and lightly rest your right hand on the support as you lift your left leg off the ground and balance it in front of you with the knee slightly bent.

b Gently swing your left leg back and forward, keeping the leg relaxed and loose and the movement controlled.

How many? Swing the leg 10 times, then repeat on the other side.

Top tips

- Don't swing the leg too high; keep it within your comfortable range of motion.
- Keep the leg relaxed at the knee all the way through the swing.
- Try to keep the rest of your body strong and still as your leg moves.
- See how much you can balance yourself; use your support very lightly.

7a

7b

8 CALF STRETCH

What for?

To stretch out the muscles in the back of your lower legs, which work hard to propel you forward when walking.

How to do it

Stand tall with your feet parallel and your hands on your hips. Take one step back with your right leg, pushing the heel into the ground, and bend your left knee, taking your weight forward onto it and placing your hands lightly on the front thigh. You should feel the stretch down the back of your right leg below the knee. Hold the stretch for 10 seconds.

How many? Perform the stretch once with each leg.

Top tips

- Keep both feet pointing forward throughout the stretch.
- Make sure your bent knee is directly above and in line with your ankle.
- Keep your back heel pushed firmly into the floor throughout the stretch.

9 ANKLE CIRCLE

What for?

To mobilize and loosen up the ankles so they feel warm and supple and ready to walk on.

How to do it

Find something to use for balance, and hold on with your right hand. With the weight on your right foot, lift your left foot a few inches off the floor and make circles.

How many? Do 5 circles in one direction, and then 5 the other way, then repeat with the other foot.

Top tips

- Circle the foot slowly, working through the full range of movement in the ankle.
- Avoid locking the knee on the supporting leg.

Your cool down

When you start your cool-down, wear an extra layer or two of clothing to avoid getting cold as your body temperature starts to drop. It's really important that your muscles stay warm while you perform your stretches, and I would suggest, if you have been walking in your neighborhood, that your cool-down walk take you back to your front door so you can do the following stretches indoors, at home. If you have driven to your walking destination, keep a towel or exercise mat in the car and use it for your stretches. However, if it is a really chilly day, it is probably a good idea to drive home before stretching—and remember to have the heater on in the car!

1 GENTLE WALKING

What for?

To allow your heart and respiration rate gradually to return to normal before you stop moving.

How to do it

Slow your walking pace down gradually, and continue walking for 5 minutes or so until you feel that your breathing and heart rate have returned to normal.

Top tips

• Concentrate on your breathing, taking deep, even breaths until your respiration rate returns to normal.

• Don't let your posture and walking technique go out of the window just because you are walking more slowly.

2 SHOULDER STRETCH

What for?

The shoulder muscles work hard when you are walking, to keep the arms pumping backward and forward at speed. This simple stretch will help to prevent them from aching too much the next day.

How to do it

Stand with your feet hip width apart and knees slightly relaxed. Reach your left arm across your chest, and place your right hand on your left elbow.

Gently ease your arm in toward your chest by applying gentle pressure with your hand. Hold the stretch for 15–30 seconds.

How many? Perform the stretch once with each arm.

Top tips

- Keep the arm at shoulder height as you perform the stretch.
- Ease into the stretch gently; don't force your arm where it doesn't want to go.
- Breathe deeply and relax into the stretch and you will find that the muscles relax, too.

2

3 CHEST STRETCH

What for?

The muscles in the chest also work in the pumping action of the arms. Opening out the chest is great for posture, too.

How to do it

a Stand with your feet hip width apart and your knees relaxed. Link your fingers together behind you, next to the small of your back.

Slowly raise your arms up behind you as far as your flexibility will allow.

3a

3b

b If you find that you are too stiff to get into this position, try the stretch without linking the fingers. Hold the stretch for 15–30 seconds, then relax.

How many? Perform the stretch just once.

Top tips

• Don't allow the body to tilt forward as the arms lift behind.

• You should feel this stretch across the front of your chest and in the front of your shoulders.

4 QUADRICEPS STRETCH

What for?

The big muscles in the front of your thighs work really hard when you are walking. Quite often you will notice them aching the next day but stretching will prevent them from feeling too sore.

How to do it

Stand sideways on to a support, with your feet together, and hold on lightly for balance with your right hand. With your weight on your right leg, lift your left foot behind you and catch hold of it with your left hand.

Bring your knees together, and push your hips slightly forward by tightening your bottom muscles so that you increase the stretch. Hold the stretch for 15–30 seconds.

How many? Perform the stretch once on each leg.

Top tips

• Keep your supporting knee slightly relaxed to avoid locking the joint.

• Keep your head up and focus forward to help you balance on one leg.

4

5a

5b

5 SPINE TWIST

What for?

To lengthen and release any tension in the spine. This is also a good stretch for general spine mobility.

How to do it

a Sit on a mat with your legs extended out in front of you. Cross the right leg over the left, bending the knee and placing the foot flat on the floor next to your left thigh or as high as feels comfortable. Extend your left arm around the bent knee and rest the hand against the outside of your right thigh.

b Using your arm as a lever, twist your spine to the right as far as possible and look behind you. Hold the stretch for 15 seconds.

How many? Perform the stretch once on each side.

Top tips

- Make sure that you are sitting upright before you start the spine twist. Once you start twisting, think of lengthening even taller as you move. You should feel as if you have grown at least an inch by the time you finish this exercise.
- If you have any back problems, be extremely careful with this stretch. Make it very small and gentle, and if it feels uncomfortable at any point, stop right away.

6 FROG STRETCH

What for?

This stretch is great for increasing flexibility in the inner thigh muscles and the hips.

How to do it

a Sit up tall with your knees bent and pointing out to the sides and the soles of your feet placed together in front of you.

b Place your hands on your ankles and rest your elbows just above your knees. Apply gentle pressure with the elbows, and ease the knees down toward the floor. Hold the stretch for 15–30 seconds, and then relax.

How many? Perform the stretch just once.

Top tips

- Hold on to your ankles rather than your feet to avoid any pulling on the feet.
- Keep the spine upright and lengthened throughout the stretch.
- Make sure that the soles of your feet are touching, from heel to toe.

6a

6b

7 BACK STRETCH

What for?

This is an effective lower-back stretch, which also opens out the chest and feels great.

How to do it

a Lie on your front with your forearms on the floor, and your chin resting on your hands. Keep your arms close to your body and your nose pointing down toward the floor.

b Push against your hands, and slowly lift the chest and shoulders away from the floor, lengthening through the spine. Lift only as far as you feel comfortable. Hold the stretch for 15–30 seconds, and then gradually lower the upper body back to the floor with control.

How many? Perform the stretch just once.

Top tips

- If you have any back problems, it is probably best to skip this exercise.
- Keep your focus down toward the floor so that you keep the head in line with the spine.
- Keep your core engaged throughout this stretch to avoid overextending the spine.

7a

7b

8 BOTTOM AND HIP STRETCH

What for?
To stretch the muscles in the bottom and the hips—great for relaxing after a long, hard walk!

How to do it
a Lie on your back with the knees bent and feet flat on the floor. Rest your right ankle over the left thigh, keeping the knee at an open angle.

b Link your fingers around your left thigh, and gently pull the leg toward your body, bringing the foot off the floor. Ease the leg in as far as feels comfortable, and hold the stretch for 15–30 seconds.

How many? Perform the stretch once with each leg.

Top tips
• Keep your tailbone pushed into the floor throughout the exercise.
• If you feel any pressure on your knee, reduce the angle at which you have crossed your legs.
• Try not to allow too much tension in the upper body as you pull the leg in.

8a

8b

9a

9b

9 SIDE-TO-SIDE STRETCH

What for?

This is a lovely, relaxing stretch—try to allow all the tension to slip away from the spine, chest, and hip area.

How to do it

a Lie on your back with your knees bent, feet flat on the floor, and your arms stretched out to the sides.

b Slowly allow your knees to lower over to the right side as far as feels comfortable, keeping both shoulders in contact with the floor. Hold the stretch for 15–30 seconds, and then slowly bring your knees back to the center.

How many? Perform the stretch once on each side.

Top tips

- Keep the movement slow and controlled throughout.
- Keep your abdominal muscles contracted and core engaged throughout the exercise to support the lower back.
- Do not move your shoulders or your chest as you move the legs.

10 RELAXATION POSE

What for?
To relax the whole body after a hard workout and allow all the tension to slip away.

How to do it
Lie on your back with your legs slightly apart and your arms resting by your sides, but slightly away from your body. Close your eyes and relax.

Take deep, even breaths, breathing in through your nose and out through your mouth. Direct the breath into your abdominals and concentrate on the stomach rising and falling with each breath.

As you breathe in, imagine the breath traveling through the body to any area of tension, and as you breathe out, think of all the tension being released. Try to clear your mind of any other thoughts. If a thought pops into your head, send it away again on a fluffy white cloud.

Stay here for as long as you can, then when you are ready, slowly open your eyes and sit up in your own time.

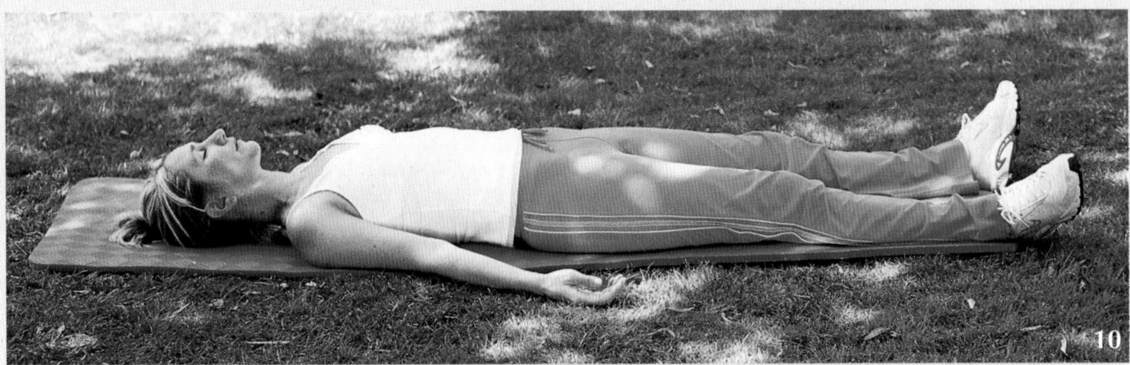
10

Stretch safely

- Always make sure you have the correct technique when stretching.
- Move gently into each stretch, giving your muscles time to relax and adjust.
- Never bounce, as this increases the risk of muscle tears and soreness. Stretching should be gradual and relaxed.
- Take a stretch only as far as your body will allow; don't try to copy others.
- Stretching should feel good. You should stretch to the point of mild discomfort, at most, and then ease up. Do not stretch until it hurts. If there's any pain, stop.
- Always make sure your muscles are warm before you stretch.
- Don't hold your breath during a stretch.
- Focus on the muscle groups you want to stretch.

HOW HARD ARE YOU WORKING?

To get the best fitness and weight-loss results from your walking, it is essential that you monitor your progress and be able to tell how hard you are working. In the beginning, your basic goal is to transform your everyday stroll into a cardiovascular power walk. However, once you have achieved this, it is important that you keep setting yourself goals that you can work towards.

In order to improve your level of fitness and ensure that you are losing weight, you need to understand the principle of "overload," which means creating a challenge for yourself and pushing your body that little bit farther each time you exercise. It is only when a walking session is more intense than the one before, when it pushes you beyond your usual capacity, that it presents a challenge which the body can respond to. In this way, the body adapts that it surpasses what it knows it can already cope with. This chapter therefore looks at how you can increase the intensity of your workout as your confidence grows.

However, in order to step up the challenge it's crucial that you are able to measure your exercise accurately. There are many different ways you can do this and some are more technical than others, but all are effective, and you should therefore experiment and find which works best for you. If your intensity level is too low, you will see little benefit from your exercise, but if it is too high you still won't get the most out of it, because you will quickly become exhausted. Monitoring yourself will show you what is a challenge, but still safe. It is the only way to take charge of your exercise program and get real results.

How to calculate your heart rate

The harder you work, the more energy your body requires—energy that is produced through the metabolism of fat stored in the body. However, this metabolic reaction depends on enough oxygen being present, and when the heart is pumping blood efficiently and quickly to the working muscles then oxygen levels are high. This direct relation between the body's ability to metabolize fat and your elevated heart rate therefore means that the latter is a very efficient gauge of how hard your body is working.

Being able to compare the intensity of one walk to the next is crucial to attaining your weight-loss goals. Here are two ways you can measure your heart rate; each is probably as accurate as the other, although one costs money and the other is free!

Heart rate monitors

Heart rate monitors are available to buy from any good sporting goods store or supplier of fitness equipment (see Resources, page 141).

I describe their capabilities in more detail on page 125, so here I'll simply say that whereas they can be a great investment, I wouldn't recommend that you rush out and buy one if you are a beginner. Treat yourself to one when you have achieved a weight-loss goal and want to step your fitness up a bit.

Taking your pulse

This is the good old-fashioned way of calculating your heart rate. There are two places where you can find your pulse: one is on your wrist (radial pulse) and the other on the side of your neck (carotid pulse).

a Your radial pulse Place your index and middle fingers on the inside of your wrist at the side underneath the base of your thumb. Apply gentle pressure and you should easily feel your pulse.

b Your carotid pulse Place your index and middle fingers on the side of your neck, underneath your jawline and just forward of your ear. Don't press too hard here, as you can affect your heart rate!

In both places, make sure that you don't use your thumb, as you have a pulse point here, too.

Once you have found your pulse, use a watch with a second hand or a stopwatch, and count how many beats you feel in the space of 20 seconds. Multiply this figure by 3 and it will give you your beats per minute.

a

b

Resting heart rate

Resting heart rate simply means the rate of a person's heart at rest. The best time to calculate yours is in the morning before you get out of bed or do anything active. Take your heart rate at the radial or carotid pulse point and, using a stopwatch or watch with a second hand, count the number of beats your heart makes over 20 seconds, then multiply by 3 to find your beats per minute. You would expect it to be somewhere between 60 and 80 beats per minute.

Resting heart rate generally rises with age, and it would be higher for a smoker. In most cases, the fitter you are, the lower your resting heart rate will be. Try taking yours now, and then again after you have been following a walking program for three months.

Training zones

The speed at which your heart beats during exercise depends on your level of fitness and your age. Training zones utilize this knowledge and provide a system of guidelines that tell you how hard your heart should be working, depending on your age and the intensity level you are working at. Look at the calculations opposite to find the maximum heart rate for your age. Exercising at that rate is extremely high intensity; and therefore as a beginner you will want to work at 50–65 percent of your maximum heart rate and work up from there, elevating your heart to the right level or "training zone" to match your goals.

Warm-up / beginners' zone = 50–65 percent of your maximum heart rate
This is the easiest zone and should be used by beginners or anyone recovering from illness or injury. Experienced walkers also often use this level for warming up and cooling down. Working in this zone carries a low risk of injury and has still been shown to lower blood pressure and cholesterol levels. A high percentage of the calories you burn when working in this zone are from fats.

Fat-burning zone = 65–75 percent of your maximum heart rate
This is the optimum zone to work in if your goal is fat burning. Once again, a high percentage of the calories burned will be from fats. Working in this zone has the health benefits described for the first zone and is also good for building endurance for longer workout sessions.

Aerobic zone = 75–85 percent of your maximum heart rate
Working in this zone will strengthen your lungs and even increase the size of your heart! This is the optimum zone to work in if you are training for an endurance event. Your body will burn a mixture of fat and glycogen (carbohydrates) for energy, although more total calories will be burned than in the previous zones.

Anaerobic zone = 85–100 percent of your maximum heart rate
Exercising at this level is usually done to improve athletic performance, and because very little fat is burned at this level, it is not recommended for weight-loss. In this zone you are using glycogen (carbohydrates) to burn for fuel, but without enough oxygen, and therefore it is no longer classed as aerobic exercise. Training in this zone will build speed for sprinting and other short, sharp bursts of energy.

Fat-burning zone—quick reference guide

Age (years)	Ideal pulse rate for fat burning	Age (years)	Ideal pulse rate for fat burning
15–19	143 beats per min.	45–49	122 beats per min.
20–24	139 beats per min.	50–54	118 beats per min.
25–29	136 beats per min.	55–59	115 beats per min.
30–34	132 beats per min.	60–64	111 beats per min.
35–39	129 beats per min.	65–69	108 beats per min.
40–44	125 beats per min.	70–75	104 beats per min.

How to calculate your personal training zones in 4 easy steps

Step 1 What is your maximum heart rate?
This is a very easy calculation. The maximum heart rate (MHR) of a baby is 220 beats per minute for a boy and 226 beats per minute for a girl. To calculate your MHR, you simply subtract your age from this figure.

The following example shows the calculation for the MHR of a 30-year-old man:
220 (MHR of male baby)
-30 (age of man)
=190 beats per minute

Step 2 Calculate your warm-up/beginners' zone
We know that when working in this zone we are aiming to work at 50–65 percent of our MHR, so if we are using the example above we need to work out 50 percent and 65 percent of 190 (MHR of a 30-year-old man):
50% of 190 = 95
65% of 190 = 124

So if a 30-year-old man wants to work in the warm-up/beginners' training zone, he should aim to keep his heart rate between 95 and 124 beats per minute.

Step 3 Calculate your fat-burning zone
If fat burning is the goal then we know we should be aiming to work at 65–75 percent of our MHR. This time I will use a 45-year-old woman as my example.

First calculate her MHR:
226 (MHR of female baby)
-45 (age of woman)
=181 beats per minute

65% of 181 = 118
75% of 181 = 136

So if a 45-year-old woman wants to work in her fat-burning training zone, she should aim to keep her heart rate between 118 and 136 beats per minute.

Step 4 Calculate your aerobic training zone
If we want to work in our aerobic training zone, we need to work at 75–85 percent of our MHR. This time try the calculation with your own age.

MHR of a baby
-your age
= _____ (your MHR)

75% of your MHR =
85% of your MHR =

To work in your aerobic training zone 1 you should keep your heart rate between __ and __ beats per minute. Try working out your other training zones now.

Other ways of judging exercise intensity

Although your heart rate is the best measure of your exercise intensity, there are other methods you can use. These are especially useful for people who do not have normal heart-rate responses to exercise, such as pregnant women, people on medication such as beta-blockers, or cardiac or diabetic patients. However, because these tests are subjective, it is advisable if possible to use them in conjunction with taking your pulse rate.

Talk test

The talk test is a straightforward, practical way of measuring how hard you are working. It is based on your ability to speak while exercising and is good at determining your comfort zone of aerobic intensity. If you are exercising at a light or moderate pace, you should be able to hold a conversation without too much trouble or strain. If you find you are too out of breath to carry on a short conversation, the activity would be considered vigorous.

If you are trying to work within your fat-burning zone you should be working at a level of intensity that allows you to breathe rhythmically and comfortably throughout your workout. This often means that you can hold a conversation with your walking partner, speaking in full sentences, but slightly slower than you would normally.

Ratings of perceived exertion (Borg scale)

This simple and quick method requires you to rate on a scale of 1–10 (see below) how hard you feel you are working, both physically and mentally. You should consider how heavy and demanding the exercise feels to you personally and take into account all feelings such as shortness of breath, muscular pain, and fatigue, rather than focusing on just one element. You should try to keep your exercise level somewhere between 4 (somewhat strong) and 6 (strong).

Assessing your RPE is a very good way of training yourself to be more body-aware. Because it is a personal scale, it's worth tracking your progress and making a note of the walking pace that you associate with each level. It's a good system for beginners, as it is so simple to use. However, bear in mind that at the start of your program you won't be so familiar with your body and you are likely to over-estimate slightly.

0	Nothing at all
0.5	Very, very weak
1	Very weak
2	Weak
3	Moderate
4	Somewhat strong
5	Strong
6	Strong
7	Very strong
8	Very strong
9	Very strong
10	Very, very strong (maximal)

CHAPTER 6

Ways of increasing the challenge

You now know how to measure your exercise intensity, and as your fitness level increases it is important that you know how to step it up so that you are pushing yourself a little further each time. No matter what type of exercise you are involved in, as your body starts to benefit from the exercise, you will find it becomes easier and you recover more quickly. This means it is time to turn up the level. You can do this in one of three ways: increase the duration, increase the frequency, or increase the intensity of your walks.

Duration

One of the easiest ways to increase your walking program is to continue walking for longer each time you go out. This sounds easy in theory, but in my experience one of the most common complaints from clients is that they lack time. You may find that if you gradually increase the duration of your walk, you adjust your lifestyle accordingly and the walk does become more important than the other pressing things you need to fit into your day!

However, if it's difficult for you to spare large chunks of time on a regular basis, try including several short walks in your day, rather than one long one. Exercise needs to be regular for you to get the best results, but it makes no difference if you make up the time in short, sharp bursts. For example, walk the kids to ballet class, or Cub Scouts, instead of taking them in the car, take the stairs instead of the elevator, or go for a walk in your lunch hour.

Frequency

Again, time may be an issue for you, but you should find it easier to go for an extra 30-minute walk each week than it is to increase each of your three 30-minute walks by 10 minutes. This works hand in hand with increasing duration, in finding other ways of adapting your lifestyle to include more walking.

Intensity

Last but not least, you can increase the intensity of your walk. The most obvious way is to start to walk faster; each session's aim should be to try to knock a bit of time off your previous record so you can cover the same distance in a shorter time. Once you can do this, you should increase the distance to use the time you have gained!

As you speed up, be careful of your technique. If you shorten your stride slightly, your legs can move faster, but make sure that the movement is still fluid and that you aren't bouncing. You will also need to lean forward a little in order to keep your balance.

Another way of increasing intensity is to walk uphill. This could be for all of your walk or just part of it. You can control how much you increase the challenge by the steepness of the gradient, but even a gentle slope can make a real difference to your heart rate (see hill walking on page 61). The temptation when you start to walk uphill is to slow down your pace, so make sure you keep your speed up!

Changing the type of surface or terrain you are walking can be an added challenge to your walk. Walking on sand is especially difficult, as it absorbs the downward motion of the foot and requires extra effort to pick up each step. However, this movement places very little stress on the joints, and so you are less prone to injury. The key thing is to keep your walks varied, for different terrains such as woodland or long grass will test the body in new and different ways.

Using your arms will also affect the intensity of your walk. You can do this by making a conscious effort to put more power into their movements, or you could try walking with poles (Nordic walking, see page 54).

A lot of people ask if they should carry hand weights when they walk. Although this would increase the intensity of your walk, I wouldn't recommend it, as it will put unnecessary pressure on the joints in your arms, playing havoc with your posture.

Ask your doctor

Before you embark on any type of exercise program, you should always have a chat with your doctor if you are in any doubt about your physical health. If any of the following apply to you, you must get their advice on how to make your exercise program safe for you.

- **Heart condition**
- **Recent surgery**
- **Chest pain**
- **Recurring fainting or dizziness**
- **Currently on medication or having medical treatment**
- **Pregnancy**
- **Diabetes**

LET'S GET WALKING

I know you are eager to get walking and start losing weight. However, before you start, it is worth pausing and deciding what your goals really are, for if these are clearly worked out, it is far easier to get motivated and stay motivated.

Goals are best when they are personal and right for you. Think how much weight you would like to lose, and give yourself a time frame in which to lose it, ideally aiming toward a date that means something to you, like a birthday, a vacation, or a similar occasion when you can celebrate your success. It is also a good idea to broaden the scope of your achievements so that you don't focus on weight-loss as your only goal. Your *Walking for Weight-Loss* program will result in all kinds of additional benefits, such as a glowing complexion, a healthier heart, deeper reserves of energy, and a more positive outlook. All these will make a real difference to your life, so include them in your goals and appreciate the changes they bring as you improve your level of fitness.

Once you have a long-term goal it is important that you break it down into manageable, step-by-step challenges. For example, saying that you are going to lose 25 lb. (11 kg) can seem quite intimidating, but if you have a weekly target of losing 1 lb. (0.4 kg) over 25 weeks, suddenly it seems realistic, and you have a reason to monitor your progress on a regular basis and feel satisfaction from each step taken in the right direction. When you are happy with your goals, it will be easy for you to select an appropriate walking program from pages 106–111. I have given you a number of choices to start with, but as you become more body-aware, you can personalize each program and customize it to your specific needs.

Setting your goals

Have a think about what is important to you, and make a note of it on the table below. Remember to keep your goals realistic; setting unachievable ones will damage your motivation and be unproductive in the long run. It really isn't worth putting yourself under so much pressure that you feel stressed out—the more you enjoy your walking program, the more you will reap the benefits.

Staying motivated

It doesn't matter how much of a dedicated walker you are, or you become, there will always be days when you just don't feel like it. You may feel tired or lazy, that you simply don't have time, or even a little despondent with a week of slow improvement. The most important thing is that you do not give up, for once you allow your program to lapse completely, it is much harder to get going again.

In fact almost half of all people who embark on an exercise program quit within three to six months, and a big percentage of these continue to pay for a health club membership even when they don't use it! The good news is that motivation slumps usually don't last too long, so you can trust that you will get it back. However, here are some ideas for giving your motivation an added boost.

Schedule your walks

This is especially important if your work is not always at set hours and you quite often find yourself scheduling after-hours meetings and appointments. At the start of each week, make a note of your walking sessions in your diary so they are there in black and white to remind you. That way you will treat them as something fixed on your "to do" list, you will feel less tempted to swap any of your walks for a drink with some friends, and you won't double-book yourself.

My goals

Short term	Date achieved	Medium term	Date achieved	Long term	Date achieved

Sign up for an event

This will give you something to work toward from the outset, as it requires a certain level of commitment. There is a good variety of charity events to choose from and it should be easy to find a walk that suits your level. The point of these events is, of course, to raise money for charity, so try to collect as much sponsorship money as you can, because not only does it benefit the charity but nobody wants to let down all their family and friends!

Find a walking buddy

One effective way of sticking to your walking program is to team up with someone who wants to walk with you. It can be hard to find someone who is at your level and has the same goals, but it is worth searching, for it will make a huge difference to your motivation. On those days when you'd like to go to the movies after work instead of going for your scheduled walk, you will have your friend to consider, and this will help you stick to your plans.

A good walking buddy will provide encouragement when your spirits are flagging and turn your walks into an enjoyable occasion. You can check how hard you are working while you are talking, for if you are walking at moderate to high intensity you should be able to carry on a conversation, though you may also be a little breathless. Take care that you don't idle as you chatter, and if it feels too easy, take it up a notch.

Vary your walk

The quickest way to get bored with your walking program is to follow the same route each time you go out. Have a few routes to vary the scenery, and keep the experience new and interesting. Variety is even good for your body, as it, too, will get used to the same old route and hills over and over again, presenting less of a challenge and so producing fewer results.

Create a list of your favorite routes and include a short walk for those days when you have only a small window of time to spare, and a particularly beautiful and energizing route for those days when you need a little lift.

Reward yourself

It is important that you acknowledge when you achieve your goals. Your rewards can be whatever you like, as long as they feel like a treat. Plan what they will be as you set your goals, so that you have something to work toward and look forward to. Some people like to plan their rewards so that they have some relevance to their fitness program. For example, you could treat yourself to a pedometer, some new walking clothing, a new pair of running shoes, or even a heart rate monitor. However, make sure you save the big rewards for the long-term goals, as this will really give you something to aspire to.

Route planning

Before you go out on your walk, you need to plan your route. Try to find places that don't have too much traffic pollution, are well lit if you are walking at night, and that you find pleasing.

Think of a landmark or point of focus for your walk, like a church or tree, as this provides a destination and means you can leave the house with a healthy sense of purpose. Make sure you are aware of any big hills or change of terrain you will come across, as these can all add to the intensity of your workout. If you do choose to include them, tackle them in the middle of the walk and certainly not at the end.

Most important, plan your route to be the distance that you want to walk, for it is extremely frustrating when, just as you are getting into your stride, the walk is over too soon. If you are road walking, drive the route in your car first and clock the distance. You can then adjust the route accordingly.

Measuring weight-loss

What is weight-loss?

The best way to lose weight is to combine your exercise program with a healthy eating plan, as time and time again it is proven that a two-pronged approach brings much better long-term results. In simple terms, losing weight means consuming fewer calories than your body uses, so if you reduce your weekly calorie-intake and increase your weekly activity level, you should find yourself well on your way to achieving your weight-loss goals.

Metabolism

Your metabolism is the process by which you convert food into energy, and the rate that your body does this at rest is referred to as your basal metabolic rate (BMR). Everybody's BMR is different, and I'm sure we all know those annoying people who eat and eat and never put on a pound! However, there are lots of factors that affect metabolism—as we age, our BMR naturally starts to slow down, and our weight, genetics, and gender all have a role to play, too.

One of the most important things to understand about your metabolism is that your body composition is a huge factor in determining your BMR, and this is something that you can change. The more muscle mass you have in your body, the faster your metabolism will be, as muscle tissue burns more calories at rest. Exercise is therefore vital not only in reducing your weight but also keeping it off.

How much to lose?

You will probably have a pretty good idea already about how overweight you are and what your ideal weight should be, but it is always a good idea to measure yourself before starting your program so that clear goals can be set.

Most of us find it easy simply to jump on the scale, but there are other ways of measuring weight, and body-fat percentage that give a more accurate picture. Try the methods below and see which works best for you. Although it is important to set your initial goals, try not to get too caught up with constant measuring; I would say once weekly or even every too weeks is enough. Most important, learn to listen to your body and how you feel, as we are all different. You may fit into the normal category in the chart, but know that you have put on 7 lb. (3 kg) and, as a result, just don't feel good.

BMI

The body mass index (BMI) is a measure of a person's body weight scaled according to height. You will often find a BMI chart in your doctor's office, and it is a useful indication of whether you need to lose or gain weight. However, bear in mind that it does have its limitations, for by simply weighing yourself you are not distinguishing between muscle and fat in your body's composition. Increased muscle mass will make you heavier, but it will also make you significantly fitter and slimmer. You can find out your BMI from some web sites, or you can calculate it for yourself:

Step 1 First have someone measure your height in meters. Let's suppose it is 1.68 meters (5 feet 6 inches).
Step 2 Multiply this figure by itself: 2.8.
Step 3 Find your weight in kilograms by dividing the pounds by 2.2. Let's say, 61 kilos (135 pounds).
Step 4 Divide the figure obtained in Step 3 by that obtained in Step 2. Result: 21.8

Categories	**BMI**
Underweight (for your height)	Less than 18.5
Healthy weight	18.5–24.9
Overweight	25–29.9
Obese	30 or greater

Measuring body-fat percentage

Because neither measuring your weight on the scale nor measuring your BMI gives a breakdown of your body composition it can mean that a person is "overweight" in the typical height-to-weight or BMI charts but actually has a low body-fat percentage. For example, a body builder's weight is much higher than average for their height and yet their body-fat percentage is very low.

If you are interested in getting an accurate measure of your fat-to-weight ratio, you should ask your family doctor or local fitness center for a test. Knowing your body-fat percentage can be a real incentive to weight-loss, because reducing it by even a few points can make a big difference to the way you look and feel. As a guideline, the average adult body-fat percentage for a woman ranges from 22 to 25 percent and the average adult body-fat percentage for a man ranges from 15 to 18 percent.

Using a tape measure

The good old tape measure is a very simple way of measuring your weight-loss progress. We all get caught up with what the scale says, yet if we're honest, it isn't how much we weigh that concerns us, but our size.

When measuring yourself, you should make sure you get the tape measure in exactly the same place each time for accurate results; it is best to measure around the widest part of each area. Good areas to measure are:

Your waist

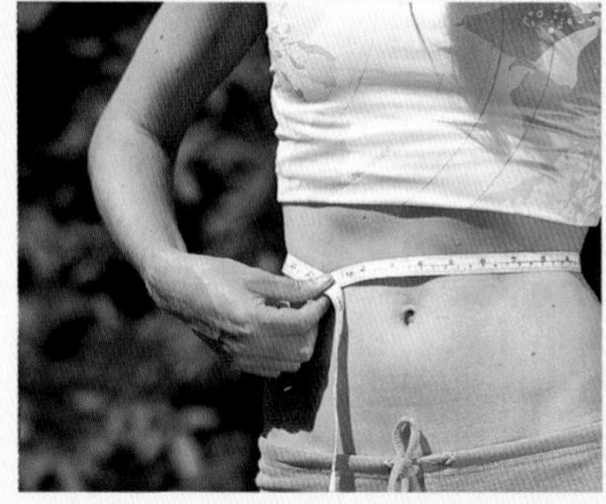

Your hips

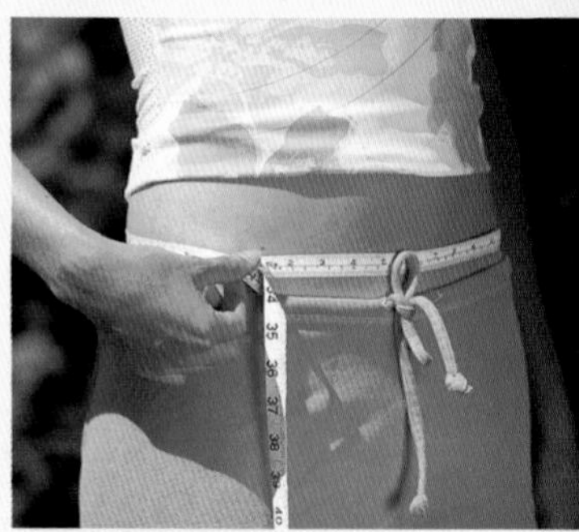

Your thigh

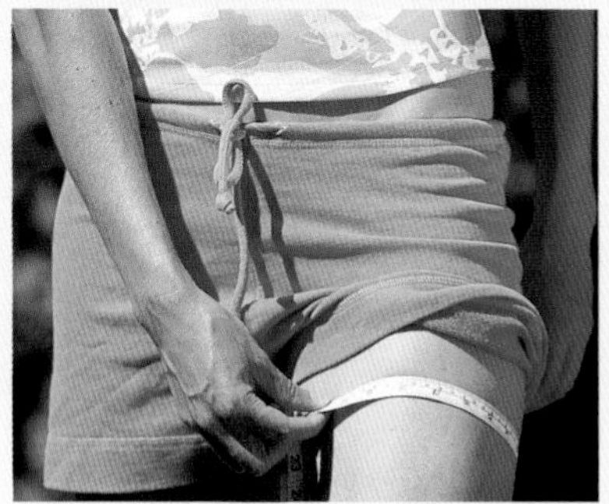

Your upper arm

The weight-loss programs

This is the perfect way to begin your weight-loss program, learning how to vary your pace and understanding the different demands it places on your body. Now is the time to get into the habit of planning a daily dose of exercise and work on good technique and posture. In just three months the results should speak for themselves.

Slow pace 50–65 percent of your maximum heart rate

Moderate pace 60–70 percent of your maximum heart rate

Faster pace 65–75 percent of your maximum heart rate (your fat-burning zone)

1. Beginners' weight-loss program

	Monday	Tuesday	Wednesday	Thursday	Friday	Saturday	Sunday
Wk 1	Walk 10 min. Moderate pace	Walk 10 min. Moderate pace	Walk 10 min. Moderate pace	Walk 10 min. Moderate pace	Walk 10 min. Moderate pace	Walk 10 min. Moderate pace	Walk 20 min. Slow pace
Wk 2	Day off, but include a walk to the stores/park, etc.	Walk 10 min. Moderate pace	Walk 15 min. Moderate pace	Walk 10 min. Moderate pace	Walk 15 min. Moderate pace	Walk 10 min. Moderate pace	Walk 30 min. Slow pace
Wk 3	Day off, but include a walk to the stores/park, etc.	Walk 15 min. Moderate pace	Walk 15 min. Moderate pace	Walk 10 min. Moderate pace	Walk 15 min. Moderate pace	Walk 15 min. Moderate pace	Walk 30 min. Slow–moderate pace
Wk 4	Day off, but include a walk to the stores/park, etc.	Walk 15 min. Moderate pace	Walk 15 min. Moderate pace	Walk 15 min. Moderate pace	Walk 10 min. Faster pace	Walk 15 min. Faster pace	Walk 30 min. Slow–moderate pace
Wk 5	Day off, but include a walk to the stores/park, etc.	Walk 15 min. Moderate pace	Walk 15 min. Faster pace	Walk 15 min. Moderate pace	Walk 15 min. Faster pace	Walk 15 min. Moderate pace	Walk 30 min. Moderate pace
Wk 6	Day off, but include a walk to the stores/park, etc.	Walk 20 min. Moderate pace	Walk 15 min. Faster pace	Walk 20 min. Moderate pace	Walk 15 min. Faster pace	Walk 20 min. Moderate pace	Walk 40 min. Slow–moderate pace
Wk 7	Day off, but include a walk to the stores/park, etc.	Walk 20 min. Moderate pace	Walk 20 min. Moderate pace	Walk 15 min. Faster pace	Walk 20 min. Moderate pace	Walk 20 min. Moderate pace	Walk 40 min. Slow–moderate pace
Wk 8	Day off, but include a walk to the stores/park, etc.	Walk 20 min. Moderate pace	Walk 20 min. Faster pace	Walk 20 min. Moderate pace	Walk 20 min. Faster pace	Walk 20 min. Moderate pace	Walk 40 min. Moderate pace
Wk 9	Day off, but include a walk to the stores/park, etc.	Walk 25 min. Moderate pace	Walk 20 min. Faster pace	Walk 25 min. Moderate pace	Walk 20 min. Faster pace	Walk 25 min. Moderate pace	Walk 40 min. Moderate pace
Wk 10	Day off, but include a walk to the stores/park, etc.	Walk 25 min. Moderate pace	Walk 20 min. Faster pace	Walk 30 min. Moderate pace	Walk 25 min. Moderate pace	Walk 25 min. Moderate pace	Walk 40 min. Moderate pace

Once you are satisfied with your technique it is time to use it to propel yourself forwards that little bit faster and improve on your walk's fat-burning potential. Choose a route that has relatively flat and even terrain so that you can concentrate on building up speed—'at speed' is walking as fast as you can while maintaining correct posture.

Moderate pace 60–70 percent of your maximum heart rate

Faster pace 65–75 percent of your maximum heart rate

At speed between 70–80 percent of your maximum heart rate

2. Intermediate weight-loss program

	Monday	Tuesday	Wednesday	Thursday	Friday	Saturday	Sunday
Wk 1	Rest day	Walk 30 min. Moderate pace	Walk 25 min. Moderate pace	Walk 30 min. Moderate pace	Walk 25 min. Moderate pace	Walk 20 min. At speed	Walk 45 min. Moderate pace
Wk 2	Rest day	Walk 30 min. Moderate pace	Walk 35 min. Moderate pace	Walk 30 min. Moderate pace	Walk 25 min. Faster pace	Walk 35 min. Moderate pace	Walk 45 min. Moderate pace
Wk 3	Rest day	Walk 30 min. Moderate pace	Walk 35 min. Moderate pace	Walk 30 min. Moderate pace	Walk 35 min. Moderate pace	Walk 25 min. At speed	Walk 50 min. Moderate pace
Wk 4	Rest day	Walk 35 min. Moderate pace	Walk 40 min. Moderate pace	Walk 35 min. Moderate pace	Walk 30 min. Faster pace	Walk 40 min. Moderate pace	Walk 50 min. Moderate pace
Wk 5	Rest day	Walk 35 min. Moderate pace	Walk 40 min. Moderate pace	Walk 35 min. Moderate pace	Walk 40 min. Moderate pace	Walk 30 min. At speed	Walk 50 min. Moderate pace
Wk 6	Rest day	Walk 40 min. Moderate pace	Walk 45 min. Moderate pace	Walk 40 min. Moderate pace	Walk 35 min. Faster pace	Walk 45 min. Moderate pace	Walk 55 min. Moderate pace
Wk 7	Rest day	Walk 35 min. Moderate pace	Walk 40 min. Moderate pace	Walk 35 min. Moderate pace	Walk 40 min. Moderate pace	Walk 30 min. At speed	Walk 55 min. Moderate pace
Wk 8	Rest day	Walk 40 min. Moderate pace	Walk 45 min. Moderate pace	Walk 40 min. Moderate pace	Walk 35 min. Faster pace	Walk 45 min. Moderate pace	Walk 55 min. Moderate pace
Wk 9	Rest day	Walk 45 min. Moderate pace	Walk 50 min. Moderate pace	Walk 45 min. Moderate pace	Walk 50 min. Moderate pace	Walk 35 min. At speed	Walk 60 min. Moderate pace
Wk 10	Rest day	Walk 45 min. Moderate pace	Walk 50 min. Moderate pace	Walk 45 min. Moderate pace	Walk 40 min. Faster pace	Walk 50 min. Moderate pace	Walk 60 min. Moderate pace

If you can feel your fitness level improving and find it quite easy to walk up a gentle hill without getting out of breath it is time to graduate to the advanced program. You don't want your fitness or weight-loss achievements to plateau and so the answer is to step up the intensity and provide new challenges for your body.

Moderate pace 60–70 percent of your maximum heart rate

Faster pace 65–75 percent of your maximum heart rate

At speed 70–80 percent of your maximum heart rate

3. Advanced weight-loss program

	Monday	Tuesday	Wednesday	Thursday	Friday	Saturday	Sunday
Wk 1	Rest day	Walk 45 min. Faster pace	Walk 50 min. Moderate pace	Walk 45 min. Faster pace	Walk 40 min. At speed	Walk 50 min. Faster pace	Walk 60 min. Moderate pace
Wk 2	Rest day	Walk 45 min. Faster pace	Walk 50 min. Faster pace	Walk 45 min. Faster pace	Walk 60 min. Moderate pace	Walk 40 min. At speed	Walk 60 min. Moderate pace
Wk 3	Rest day	Walk 50 min. Faster pace	Walk 55 min. Moderate pace	Walk 50 min. Faster pace	Walk 45 min. At speed	Walk 55 min. Faster pace	Walk 70 min. Moderate pace
Wk 4	Rest day	Walk 50 min. Faster pace	Walk 55 min. Faster pace	Walk 50 min. Faster pace	Walk 70 min. Moderate pace	Walk 45 min. At speed	Walk 70 min. Moderate pace
Wk 5	Rest day	Walk 55 min. Faster pace	Walk 60 min. Moderate pace	Walk 55 min. Faster pace	Walk 50 min. At speed	Walk 60 min. Faster pace	Walk 70 min. Moderate pace
Wk 6	Rest day	Walk 55 min. Faster pace	Walk 60 min. Faster pace	Walk 55 min. Faster pace	Walk 70 min. Moderate pace	Walk 50 min. At speed	Walk 70 min. Moderate pace
Wk 7	Rest day	Walk 55 min. Faster pace	Walk 60 min. Moderate pace	Walk 55 min. Faster pace	Walk 50 min. At speed	Walk 60 min. Faster pace	Walk 80 min. Moderate pace
Wk 8	Rest day	Walk 55 min. Faster pace	Walk 60 min. Faster pace	Walk 55 min. Faster pace	Walk 80 min. Moderate pace	Walk 50 min. At speed	Walk 80 min. Moderate pace
Wk 9	Rest day	Walk 60 min. Faster pace	Walk 70 min. Moderate pace	Walk 60 min. Faster pace	Walk 55 min. At speed	Walk 70 min. Faster pace	Walk 80 min. Moderate pace
Wk 10	Rest day	Walk 60 min. Faster pace	Walk 70 min. Faster pace	Walk 60 min. Faster pace	Walk 80 min. Moderate pace	Walk 55 min. At speed	Walk 80 min. Moderate pace

Long-distance training program **(see next page)**

You may have decided that one of your medium-term goals, as part of your weight-loss program, is to walk a long-distance event such as a half marathon or even a marathon. Use the program on page 110 as a guide, and adapt it to your own needs or distances, bearing in mind that your goal in long-distance training is to build up your stamina and strength over increasing distances, and then to begin to work on your speed as your fitness level improves. You should start with a goal of walking at a minimum speed of 1 mile (1.6 kilometers) in 20 minutes.

Walking-for-improved-health program **(see page 111)**

Exercise is one of the most important things we can do to improve our overall health and well-being. Lack of exercise and obesity tend to go hand in hand, and these are two of the major risk factors to our good health. The aim of the program on page 111 is to reduce stress, lower your blood pressure, and strengthen your heart and lungs. Your heart is a muscle, and, just like other muscles in your body, it needs to be exercised regularly to keep it in tip-top condition; it is even possible to increase the size of your heart muscle through exercise. Heart disease is one of the biggest causes of death in the U.S. today, and yet something as simple as walking can really help to protect you against it.

Walking not only has major benefits for your physical health but can also help improve your mental well-being. At times, stress can feel overwhelming, and setting aside some time to go for a walk can help you feel more in control of your life and give you the opportunity to get things into perspective. Exercise makes the body release its own antidepressants, endorphins, which have been proven to play a key role in reducing symptoms of anxiety, stress, and depression. Try to find a peaceful environment to walk in—even if you live in the centre of town you are likely to have a park nearby or some quieter residential streets away from busy roads.

This program will provide a satisfying challenge for anyone who wants to set themselves a goal to work towards like a race or a charity fundraiser. However, at this level it is vital that your posture and technique are exemplary as the last thing you want is an injury to halt your progress. Check your walking style at regular intervals to be safe.

Moderate pace 60–70 percent of your maximum heart rate

Faster pace 65–75 percent of your maximum heart rate

At speed 70–80 percent of your maximum heart rate

4. Long-distance training program

	Monday	Tuesday	Wednesday	Thursday	Friday	Saturday	Sunday
Wk 1	2 miles (3km) Moderate pace	Rest day	3 miles (5km) Moderate pace	2 miles (3km) Faster pace	20 min. of another activity	1 mile (1.6km) At speed	3 miles (5km) Moderate pace
Wk 2	20 min. of another activity	2 miles (3km) Faster pace	3 miles (5km) Moderate pace	Rest day	3 miles (5km) Moderate pace	2 miles (3km) Faster pace	3 miles (5km) Moderate pace
Wk 3	3 miles (5km) Moderate pace	Rest day	4 miles (6.5km) Moderate pace	3 miles (5km) Faster pace	20 min. of another activity	1½ miles (2.5km) At speed	4 miles (6.5km) Moderate pace
Wk 4	20 min. of another activity	3 miles (5km) Faster pace	4 miles (6.5km) Moderate pace	Rest day	4 miles (6.5km) Moderate pace	3 miles (5km) Faster pace	4 miles (6.5km) Moderate pace
Wk 5	3½ miles (5.5km) Moderate pace	Rest day	4½ miles (7km) Moderate pace	4 miles (6.5km) Faster pace	20 min. of another activity	2 miles (3km) At speed	5 miles (8km) Moderate pace
Wk 6	20 min. of another activity	4 miles (6.5km) Faster pace	4½ miles (7km) Moderate pace	Rest day	4½ miles (7km) Moderate pace	4 miles (6.5km) Faster pace	6 miles (9.5km) Moderate pace
Wk 7	5 miles (8km) Moderate pace	Rest day	6 miles (9.5km) Moderate pace	3½ miles (5.5km) Faster pace	20 min. of another activity	2½ miles (4km) At speed	6 miles (9.5km) Moderate pace
Wk 8	20 min. of another activity	4 miles (6.5km) Faster pace	6 miles (9.5km) Moderate pace	Rest day	4 miles (6.5km) Faster pace	4 miles (6.5km) Faster pace	8 miles (13km) Moderate pace
Wk 9	6 miles (9.5km) Moderate pace	Rest day	7 miles (11km) Moderate pace	4 miles (6.5km) Faster pace	20 min. of another activity	3 miles (5km) Faster pace At speed	6 miles (9.5km) Moderate pace
Wk 10	20 min. of another activity	5 miles (8km) Faster pace	6 miles (9.5km) Moderate pace	Rest day	4 miles (6.5km) Faster pace	4 miles (6.5km) Faster pace	10 miles (16km) Moderate pace

This is a great way to stimulate the release of endorphins, the body's natural mood enhancers. This program is slightly less intense than the previous training and weight-loss targeted programs but it is still guaranteed to improve your fitness and will give you an invaluable opportunity to work through any thoughts that have been playing on your mind.

Moderate pace 60–70 percent of your maximum heart rate

Faster pace 65–75 percent of your maximum heart rate

At speed 70–80 percent of your maximum heart rate

5. Walking-for-improved-health program

	Monday	Tuesday	Wednesday	Thursday	Friday	Saturday	Sunday
Wk 1	Spend at least 10 min. of your day walking somewhere	Walk 15 min. Moderate pace	Walk 10 min. Faster pace	As Monday	Walk 15 min. Moderate pace	Walk 10 min. Faster pace	Walk 20 min. Slow–moderate pace
Wk 2	Spend at least 10 min. of your day walking somewhere	Walk 15 min. Moderate pace	Walk 10 min. Faster pace	As Monday	Walk 15 min. Moderate pace	Walk 15 min. Faster pace	Walk 20 min. Slow–moderate pace
Wk 3	Spend at least 10 min. of your day walking somewhere	Walk 20 min. Moderate pace	Walk 15 min. Faster pace	As Monday	Walk 15 min. Moderate pace	Walk 15 min. Faster pace	Walk 30 min. Slow–moderate pace
Wk 4	Spend at least 10 min. of your day walking somewhere	Walk 20 min. Moderate pace	Walk 15 min. Faster pace	As Monday	Walk 15 min. Moderate pace	Walk 20 min. Faster pace	Walk 30 min. Slow–moderate pace
Wk 5	Spend at least 10 min. of your day walking somewhere	Walk 25 min. Moderate pace	Walk 20 min. Faster pace	As Monday	Walk 20 min. Moderate pace	Walk 15 min. At speed	Walk 30 min. Moderate pace
Wk 6	Spend at least 10 min. of your day walking somewhere	Walk 25 min. Moderate pace	Walk 20 min. Faster pace	As Monday	Walk 20 min. Moderate pace	Walk 20 min. Faster pace	Walk 40 min. Moderate pace
Wk 7	Spend at least 10 min. of your day walking somewhere	Walk 25 min. Moderate pace	Walk 20 min. Faster pace	As Monday	Walk 20 min. Moderate pace	Walk 15 min. At speed	Walk 40 min. Moderate pace
Wk 8	Spend at least 10 min. of your day walking somewhere	Walk 25 min. Moderate pace	Walk 20 min. Faster pace	As Monday	Walk 20 min. Moderate pace	Walk 20 min. Faster pace	Walk 45 min. Moderate pace
Wk 9	Spend at least 10 min. of your day walking somewhere	Walk 30 min. Moderate pace	Walk 25 min. Faster pace	As Monday	Walk 30 min. Moderate pace	Walk 15 min. At speed	Walk 55 min. Slow–moderate pace
Wk 10	Spend at least 10 min. of your day walking somewhere	Walk 30 min. Moderate pace	Walk 25 min. Faster pace	As Monday	Walk 30 min. Moderate pace	Walk 20 min. At speed	Walk 60 min. Slow–moderate pace

Walking meditation

Walking alone can really be a great pleasure. It gives you the opportunity of doing something just for yourself, when you can reflect on the comings and goings of a busy day or week and recharge your batteries. Problems are always much easier to solve after a good dose of fresh air, and as you get into the natural rhythms of your power walk, you can turn the issue over in your mind until you come up with a solution.

Being outside in beautiful surroundings is also often inspiring. If you need to come up with ideas for a presentation at work, or even for a party you are planning, hold the image in your mind and the thoughts should start to flow. However, don't forget to take a notepad so you can write them down—when you read them back I guarantee you will surprised by how clearly and creatively you were thinking.

Walking alone is also a good opportunity to try your hand at meditation. You may associate meditation with people sitting around on the floor with their legs crossed, making a rather strange humming sound, and generally not doing very much at all. But you are wrong: meditation is mental exercise for the mind in the same way that we have physical exercise for the body. It provides a buffer zone between you and the stresses of everyday life and by practicing it regularly you can strengthen your immune system and become calmer and generally more healthy in every respect.

There are many different meditation techniques and traditions, but they all have one aim in common: not to teach you how to think but how to focus your attention so that your thoughts are no longer scattered or undirected. It doesn't mean that you are unconscious; you are just trying to let go of the thousands of details that pass frenziedly through your mind.

You will be surprised to find how hard it is "just to be" in meditation, but if you can stop worrying about getting things done and allow any thoughts that enter your mind simply to pass straight through, you will be amazed at the benefits.

Walking meditation is excellent for those times when you just need a little space and the chance to be by yourself. Try it for yourself and see. . . .

WALKING MEDITATION

How to do it

1 Choose somewhere beautiful and tranquil for your walk. Start walking at an easy pace, and then try to match your breaths to your steps. Don't force a rhythm that doesn't feel right to you; try taking two steps to every breath in, and two to every breath out, allowing the momentum to lull you into a relaxed state of awareness.

2 Once you feel relaxed, turn your attention to your feet. Feel them as they make contact with the ground, feel the weight as it is transferred along the foot to propel you forward. Are you slamming your foot into the ground, or are you placing it down gently? Can you hear the crunch of earth or twigs under your feet? Become aware of your senses and your surroundings—the wind on your face, the quality of the light, the sounds, and the smells.

3 In your mind, tell yourself what you are doing: for example, "I am walking down this country lane." Keep repeating this phrase in your mind, not monotonously, but to remind yourself to experience the present moment. Whenever your mind starts to wander away from your actual walking experience, bring it back to your chosen statement, and pay attention again.

4 As you walk, keep checking that you are matching your breaths to your steps. Be mindful of your body and how it feels. Abolish any thoughts of destination, so that only the walking remains. Tune in to a specific sound and replay it in your mind. It may be birdsong or a couple of lines of overheard conversation you pick up in passing, or the sound of the wind through the trees. Then try focusing on a stationary object, and keep the image in your mind for as long as you can after it has passed. Make contact with nature again—it will energize and stimulate your soul.

How long?

Walk for at least 20 minutes and up to an hour.

GETTING THE GEAR

Before you get out there and start walking, it is useful to consider the clothing, footwear, and accessories that are available to buy, for having the right gear and feeling prepared will give you the confidence to achieve your goals wherever you are walking. One of the benefits of power walking is that it doesn't require anything too specialized, apart from a really good pair of shoes that will give you support and cushioning. However, you should still put thought into what you wear for certain weather conditions, for there are plenty of products on the market to keep you warmer, cooler, drier, and so on. Never underestimate basic comfort value—chafing materials and sore blisters can set you back weeks at a time, so always go for styles that are nonrestrictive and lightweight.

There are also various pieces of equipment like pedometers and heart rate monitors that, although not strictly necessary, can prove very useful to your walking program. In fact, a research study recently proved that gadgets like these encourage people to stay motivated by adding interest to their workouts and providing instantaneous and accurate feedback.

If you are planning to go for long walks, or to walk off the beaten track or in unpredictable conditions, it is particularly important that you wear the appropriate clothing and take supplies. Food, water, and a full first-aid kit are the essential basics, and it may also be useful to carry a small amount of money and a cellphone. If you are planning to go far, inform someone who is staying behind of your route and the time you expect to be back, and always have layers of clothing in reserve in case the weather takes a turn for the worse.

Walking shoes

Walking shoes are your most important investment for your new walking activities, because not only will a good pair make walking more comfortable and aid your technique, but they will also protect your body from injury and keep you walking for years to come.

The good news is that buying a decent shoe for walking doesn't necessarily mean having to choose the most expensive pair in the store, as generally these are high fashion and technically not that great anyway. However, don't scrimp, either. Have a good look around before you buy, and ask the sales assistant, who should be able to give you specialist advice.

Can I use my running shoes?
Different activities make different demands and so it is essential to buy shoes that are designed for a particular purpose. Running shoes are generally high at the heel to control the motion of the rear foot; this feature is not necessary for walking and only causes you to overwork the shin muscles, quickly resulting in soreness and inflammation.

Running shoes are also stiff at the toe to make the heel-to-toe running motion more efficient and to protect the feet from rocks, tree roots, and other obstacles on the ground that you don't see when moving at speed. However, walking shoes should be flexible at the toe, so they can push off easily, and cushioned at the heel, since this is where a walker lands and then rolls through the step. Don't be tempted to use your old running shoes: they won't do you any favors!

What to look for

There are thousands of walking shoes on the market, and this checklist of key features should help you weed out the high-fashion gimmicks and focus on exactly what you need.

- **A lightweight and breathable shoe. The last thing you want is a heavy, clunky, leather walking shoe.**
- **Flexibility. A walker's foot hits the ground heel first and then rolls gradually from heel to toe. So you will need a flexible sole with more bend in the toe than in a runner's shoe. You should be able to twist and bend the toe area.**
- **Good cushioning at the heel and the ball of the foot.**
- **A rounded toe box so you have room to move.**
- **A low, supportive heel that rounds (or bevels) in. A thick heel or one that flares out will cause your foot to slap down rather than roll. This slows down forward momentum and increases the likelihood of sore shins.**
- **A supported arch.**

breathable
material
rounded
toe box
low
heel
supportive
arch
flexible
sole

What about walking boots?

Walking boots are not suitable for power walking. They have a stiff sole and firm ankle support, which are great for walking on rugged terrain and stopping you from turning your ankle, but for power walking they are inflexible and heavy, and you would find them extremely uncomfortable.

What type of feet do I have?

The key features listed on the preceding page are a very good place to start when shopping for a walking shoe. However, everyone's feet are different, and the best shoe for you is one that gives you the proper support, flexibility, and cushioning and also compensates for the various idiosyncrasies of your particular posture and walking style. For example, when the heel strikes the ground, the foot, and in particular the heel and arch, will roll as part of a natural cushioning mechanism. This is called pronation.

However, some feet can roll inward too much (called over-pronation) or not enough (supination), and both can lead to painful shins and joints and even to injury. If you go to a specialist sports equipment store, you should find a shoe-fitting expert who can analyze your foot type and select a shoe that is best for your walking distance, speed, style, and surface, as well as your weight and stride.

Over-pronation

When you walk, the foot is designed to roll in slightly after landing to help disperse the shock, but over-pronators roll excessively inward. This in turn causes too much movement in the foot and the lower leg and, if not corrected with the right shoes, can lead to injury.

How to diagnose

If you are being fitted by a shoe expert they will watch your feet closely as you walk to see if you are rolling inward. Another way to find out is by placing an old pair of walking shoes on a table and looking at them from behind at eye level. Look to see if the shoe caves markedly inward and if the outer soles have worn down along the inside of the ball of the foot. Over-pronators also tend to have flat feet.

How to remedy

Look for a straight-shaped shoe that provides support for the inside of the foot and therefore helps to prevent the inward roll. You may need to go for a motion control shoe, which has firm midsoles and external control features that limit pronation. Avoid shoes with too much padding, as these can sometimes make pronation worse.

Supination

Supination, also known as under-pronation, is the opposite of over-pronation and therefore means rolling the foot too much toward the outside edge when walking. This can cause injury to the knee and Achilles tendon (at the back of the ankle) if not corrected with the right footwear.

How to diagnose
Place your shoes on a flat surface and bring your eyes level with the soles. This time you are looking to see if the outside edge of the shoe has become over-stretched and worn, even to the point of visibly tilting outward. Supination often occurs in feet with high arches.

How to remedy
Supinators tend to have quite rigid feet, so look for a shoe that is lightweight and has good flexibility on its inside edge. Also look for a curved-shape shoe: when you turn the shoe upside down and look at it, the top of the shoe will curve inward. Lastly, look for good ankle and heel support.

Plenty of room

Always make sure that there is plenty of room in your walking shoes, as footwear that's too small can cause all kinds of problems.

Walking shoes, like most sports shoes, tend to be made quite small. Bear this in mind when you are trying on shoes, because you may have to go one or even two sizes larger than you normally wear.

A few years ago, a study by the American Podiatric Medical Association revealed that most foot problems among women were a direct result of wearing too-small shoes.

Neutral feet
If you have neutral feet, your feet don't roll excessively inward or outward as you walk. When you performed the test with your shoes as described above you will have noticed that there was no marked over-stretching on either side of the sole. It will make buying shoes a little easier, but you should still look for the basic walking-shoe features.

Where to buy
Although it is great to know a bit about your feet and the way you walk, it is always a good idea to find a specialist to analyze your gait and fit your shoes accordingly. Look for the technical shoe store in your area, one that caters to serious runners and walkers. The assistants will almost certainly be trained to recommend the right shoe for you, rather than the most expensive or fashionable. If you are having trouble locating a store, first try Resources, on pages 141, or contact your local running/walking club and ask who they find reliable.

Shoe-trying tips

• When you walk, your feet swell, so always try shoes at the end of the day when feet are more swollen, or straight after a walk.

• Try the shoes on with the workout socks you will be wearing when walking.

• If you have one foot larger than the other, always buy shoes that fit the larger foot.

• Make sure there is at least a thumb's width of space between the end of your shoe and your longest toe (usually the big toe), as this will allow space for your feet to swell. The shoe should be wide enough in the toe so that your toes can move freely. Your heel should not slip, and the shoe should not pinch or bind, especially across the arch or ball of your foot. And remember to measure when you're standing up, rather than sitting down.

• Make sure you move around the store in the shoes and get the feel of them properly. And don't feel embarrassed—it's important you know that the heel doesn't slip when you jump around and that you have space to wiggle your toes at the end.

• If you can feel a rough spot in the shoe, don't be tempted to think you can wear the shoe in—it will only give you blisters. In fact, no sports footwear should need to be "worn in"; comfort value is crucial to your performance and walking shoes especially should feel good from the start.

How long should they last?

Once you're happy with your shoes, the next step is to determine how long to wear them—and it's useful to bear in mind that many walkers neglect to replace their shoes before they lose their effectiveness and often suffer chronic foot pain as a result. Keep track of how much distance you have put on your shoes, and replace them every 300–600 miles (175–375 kilometers).

If you are wearing very lightweight shoes, are overweight, or know you are hard on shoes in general, replace them slightly more frequently. You can tell when it's time to get new shoes because the shoe will have no spring left in it, a sign that the cushioning has worn out. When this has happened, lose no time in replacing them, for cushioning is essential for shock absorption and preventing injury.

Also inspect the inside of your shoes on a regular basis for seams or worn areas that might produce friction and lead to painful blisters. In order to get more life out of your shoes, wear them only for your walks, and, if possible, rotate with a second pair to give each one time to "bounce back" between walks.

CHAPTER 8

Socks

Good socks are as important as good walking shoes because the wrong kind lead to blisters and much pain. The most important job of your sock is to wick sweat away from your feet, for otherwise the skin absorbs the moisture, becoming soft, tender, and more likely to rub uncomfortably against your socks and shoes. Avoid cotton and wool socks, since these tend to absorb moisture and can cause severe blisters once they get wet.

It is also important to avoid low-cut ankle socks, for although they can look great, they won't give any protection to your Achilles tendon against the back of your shoe. And don't wear socks that are too worn: thin areas and holes are very likely to produce hot spots and blisters. There are many different brands, shapes, and materials on the market to choose from, so here's your guide to finding the best kind for you.

If you are choosing thin socks, make sure they are seamless and made of synthetic fibers to avoid any rubbing.

Thick padded socks can be good, as they have extra padding in the areas where you may normally experience chafing. Make sure you take them with you when buying shoes, though, as they can easily add half a size to your foot measurement.

Double-layered socks have two layers of material that are designed to prevent blisters, by the layers rubbing together rather than your sock against your foot. Some people find these work well for them, whereas others don't.

Another option is to wear a silk sock liner under your regular sock, which acts in the same way as the double-layered sock. These can be bought from most sporting goods stores. Select socks that fit your foot without being too tight or too loose—excess material easily bunches up and produces extra friction.

Cold-weather clothing

Layering your clothing is the way to keep warm in cold weather, as warm air gets trapped between each layer and therefore provides excellent insulation. It also means that you always have enough clothing, but never too much, and if you choose breathable and wicking fabrics, your body will be able to shed excess heat and sweat while still feeling dry.

The first layer is the base layer. This should always be made of a synthetic fabric, which draws the sweat away from the skin so it can evaporate and cool you without making you feel wet and clammy. The second layer adds warmth but also leaves you with the option of taking it off as you warm up. This insulating layer could be a long-sleeved T-shirt and fitness tights or a fleece jacket and some tracksuit bottoms. Fabrics include wool, fleece, pile, or down, but be careful to make your choice according to the weather, and allow for the fact that you will warm up during exercise—save the down vest for truly cold days.

The final, outer layer protects you from the elements and can also be removed as you warm up. The best option is a wind- and waterproof jacket that can be worn loosely, and which allows your skin to breathe;

materials like Gore-Tex are good. It will be more expensive than a raincoat, yet is a worthwhile investment, since it won't trap your perspiration in your clothing but allow it to evaporate, and also keep the rain off you.

In very cold weather you may need to wear a hat and gloves too. You can lose 30 percent of body heat through your head, so a hat can really make a difference. As you warm up, you may need to take a layer off to avoid overheating, but make sure you replace it again if you start to feel cool.

Warm-weather clothing

In a warm season or climate you will probably need just one layer of clothing, and a pair of shorts and a T-shirt always work well. It is a good idea to wear light colors and synthetic fabrics, such as Dryflo or Coolmax that are designed to allow your skin to breathe. They are also much better at preventing chafing than cotton, which retains your sweat and doesn't release it to evaporate. If the sun is shining, wear a hat to protect yourself from sunstroke, and always make sure you protect your skin with a high-factor sunscreen.

Sports bra

It's no good putting all this thought into clothing if what's underneath is uncomfortable and unsupportive. It doesn't matter what age, shape, or size you are, if you are a woman you should be wearing a sports bra, for if you continually exercise in an unsupportive bra, you will end up with very droopy breasts, and once the tissue is damaged there is no going back!

It is really important that the bra fit you properly, so if you are not sure, go and get fitted at a sporting goods store or lingerie department. Look for thick straps that won't cut into your skin; in my opinion, the best bras are those that pull on over your head with a T-back that fits round the muscles in your back. Sports bras come in varying levels of support—the bigger your cup size, the more support you will need.

Equipment

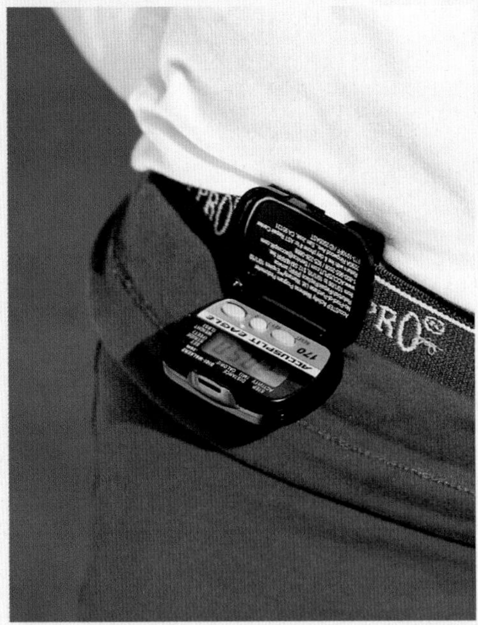

Pedometer

I thoroughly recommend that you treat yourself to a pedometer as part of your weight-loss program, as this piece of equipment will allow you to monitor your progress and provide you with motivation constantly to improve your performance.

You wear the pedometer by clipping or tying it to your waist in line with your knee, where it will register each time you take a step. Some models simply count steps, but others also allow you to program in your stride length and will then calculate distance covered and calories burned (see page 106). Set yourself a goal of distance or steps for each day, and keep a diary of your totals. The recommended number of steps is 6,000 for health and 10,000 for weight-loss, when you count all your steps during the day. In order to meet the weight-loss target, it is recommended that you go for a long, uninterrupted walk of 4,000–6,000 steps each day.

You can get a pedometer for as little as $10; most good ones cost about $30 or more. The more expensive models have extra features, some of which can be quite useful, like calorie estimators, clocks, timers, stopwatches and speed estimators, seven-day memory, and pulse-rate readers, but I would advise getting something in the middle price range (there is a slight question mark over the accuracy of the extremely cheap ones). Pedometers do, however, work best on fairly flat ground, and are not as accurate when you are walking over rough terrain.

Heart rate monitor

A heart rate monitor is a great piece of equipment, for it tells you exactly how hard you are working, and this can be invaluable when calculating your training zone for your weight-loss program (see page 92). The monitor takes a reading from a band that you wear around your chest, which measures the electrical activity of your heart with a radio signal and sends the data to a watch that you wear on your wrist and can therefore read easily. You don't need to interrupt your workout to check your heart rate, and so it becomes much easier to adjust your intensity level if you find that your heart rate is too high or low.

Be safe

• For road walking, wear reflective clothing such as a vest or an armband, so that you can be clearly seen by oncoming traffic.

• Road-test new routes with a friend to check they are not deserted or overgrown.

• Take a cellphone with you, but also carry a little money, in case you need to use a pay phone.

• Don't use a personal stereo when out walking alone, as you need to be alert to your surroundings and able to react fast.

• Trust your instincts. If you feel that something is not right, act immediately.

• If you are walking alone, carry a whistle or alarm with you for peace of mind. (Some pedometers are made with an alarm device.)

• Look confident. Walk with good posture and your head up. Acknowledge other walkers discreetly so they know you are unfazed by their presence.

• Carry ID and medical details with you.

• Don't wear a lot of visible jewelery.

The simplest monitors often don't do much more than this, other than tell you how long you've been exercising, but the hi-tech ones can also calculate calorie expenditure, average heart rate per session, percentage of calories burned as fat, and much more. Therefore, a heart rate monitor is a good way of measuring your fitness level because, as it improves, your working and resting heart rates will drop.

Nonetheless, a monitor can be quite expensive, and there are other ways of monitoring your heart rate (see pages 90–1). I suggest that you invest in one only after you have been walking for a while and are keen to monitor the intensity of your program.

Belt bag

Most people hate having to carry things in their hands and in their pockets when they go out walking, but they still need to carry a few things (such as keys, money and a cellphone). Belt bags, bum bags, or fanny packs, as they are sometimes called, are a really good solution and some bags are designed with a specific space for all these items—you can even clip your pedometer to them.

If you do wear one, make sure that it fits snugly around your waist with the bulk of the bag sitting in the small of your back. You don't want it to move around every time you take a step, or it will drive you crazy by the end of your walk!

Knapsack

I wouldn't recommend that you carry a knapsack when power walking, as it can play havoc with your posture and generally be very uncomfortable. However, you will need to take a knapsack to carry your extra clothing and provisions if you are planning to go trail or hill walking. Look for one that fits comfortably over your shoulders, and doesn't bob up and down when you move. If your walk is going to involve an overnight stay, then you may have to take a backpack, which is a larger version of the knapsack and has a frame attached. This should also have a waist/hip strap to distribute the weight evenly and take the full load off your shoulders.

Hydration pack

A hydration pack is a drinking device that looks a bit like a small knapsack. You wear it on your back in the same way, but it contains an internal bladder that you can fill with water or juice. There is a straw that protrudes from the pack and is long enough to reach over your shoulder to your mouth, enabling you to take sips without breaking your stride. This is great for long-distance walks, and some packs even have space to store a few of your other belongings.

Water bottle

You should always take water with you to stay hydrated when out walking. You can simply take the bottle your water came in, or buy a reusable bottle, which is often designed for sports purposes. It is good to have a bottle with a sports cap for ease of drinking when moving and a molded-grip shape for easy handling. Some belt bags come with a bottle holder that clips onto your waistband and leaves your hands and arms free.

Stay hydrated

Water is absolutely essential to your health and performance when exercising, for as soon as your internal temperature starts to rise through exercise, you start perspiring. This is how the body eliminates toxins and regulates its temperature, but if we don't replace this lost fluid by drinking, we will eventually become dehydrated.

First signs of dehydration

- Diminished performance due to lack of oxygen to the muscles
- Tiredness
- Dizziness
- Nausea
- Headache

Preventive measures

- Don't wait until you're thirsty to drink water, for by this time you are already dehydrated.
- Drink small amounts frequently throughout the duration of your walk.
- Be aware that on a hot day you will need to consume even more fluids.
- Check the color of your urine. It should be almost clear and not yellow or dark in color, and there should be plenty of it.
- If you drink caffeinated or alcoholic beverages, remember that these have a dehydrating effect on the body, so always match each drink with a glass of water.

Map and compass

A comprehensive map of the area where you are walking is always invaluable, especially if you are covering new ground, as it will show useful features such as rights of way and give you an accurate estimate of distance. Consider taking a compass, too, but make sure you know how to use it and have practiced with it on a simple route, or you could end up getting yourself even more lost!

First-aid kit

If you are planning a long-distance walk over difficult terrain, and especially if you are going to be camping out, you should always pack a comprehensive first-aid kit. Its contents do depend slightly on the kind of walk you are undertaking, as it makes no sense weighing yourself down with items that you won't need. However, always run down a checklist and ask yourself if you need a flashlight, flares, splints, a bandage, etc. A pocket-sized first-aid kit is something that you should take with you on any walk, regardless of length and intensity. Make sure that it contains the following:

- Plasters
- Adhesive dressing strip
- Antiseptic wipes
- Antiseptic cream
- Elastic bandage
- Eye pad with bandage
- Scissors (blunt-pointed)
- Safety pins
- Whistle
- First-aid guidance leaflet

Where to shop

Internet

The Internet is a very convenient way to shop, and you have the advantage of searching through stores worldwide to find the best product or the best deal without ever leaving your chair. However, I would recommend using this method only when you know exactly what it is you need, as the downside is that there is no expert advice on hand to help you decide between brands; also, you can't fully examine or try on the product before buying.

Specialist stores

These are fantastic when buying walking gear, whether shoes or a water bottle. They have very knowledgeable staff and are, of course, much more likely to stock the correct item rather than a high-fashion lookalike. I would especially recommend tracking down one of these stores to buy your shoes, because the staff will be able to help you find the right pair for your feet, which will be of real benefit in the long term.

Mail order

You will find that a lot of the well-known outdoor-clothing companies have a mail-order catalog. This is great to keep at home and browse through in your own time before you buy, but even if you find the product you are after, go down to the store to try it on. For recommended outlets, see Resources (page 141).

A HEALTHY DIET

CHAPTER 9

Exercise and a healthy diet go hand in hand in any weight-loss program. I am a true believer, though, that a healthy diet is for life and that we should find a balance between good and evil! I do not recommend embarking on a strict calorie-controlled regime or any other of the millions of faddy diets out there on the market. These are quick-fix answers and therefore unsustainable.

The food we eat should provide us with all the nutrients our body needs to grow, repair, and function at peak efficiency with energy and vitality. Eating the right foods is what it is all about, for it is when we start feeding our body with foods with no real nutritional value that the problems start. These foods tend to contain excess sugar, salt, fat, and chemicals that our body has no use for but which pile up the calories nonetheless.

If you want to lose weight, the important thing is not to consume more calories than you can expend in daily activity. However, as you are increasing your energy expenditure through your walking program, it is very important to keep eating, as cutting down too much on food will leave you feeling lethargic and unable to exercise properly.

Make changes to your diet by substituting fresh fruit and vegetables, quality proteins and unrefined carbohydrates for fat, starches, and refined sugars. Water is also a vital part of your diet, so drink a lot and often. Dehydration is often mistaken for hunger pangs, so don't be fooled! The good news is that once you cut back on sugary, fatty foods, your body will stop demanding them and start craving healthy foods instead. Provide your body with what it needs, and it will repay you by lifting your mood and giving you more energy and a wonderful healthy glow. And of course your weight will stabilize at what is healthy for your build, sex, and age, and you can tone and hone this slimmer physique through exercise.

Eat breakfast!

With the walking program we want to lose weight but without sacrificing any of the energy that enables us to live and exercise at our peak efficiency. The solution is simple—always eat breakfast! This is absolutely the most vital meal of the day, for after we have been asleep all night, our metabolism has slowed to slumber mode, and we need to eat to let it know it is time to wake up and speed up to be ready for the day ahead.

It is also important that we choose the right foods for breakfast, for by eating healthily first thing in the morning, we are much less likely to have an unhealthy craving for a calorie-laden meal later on. Try to include some complex carbohydrates, or low-fat protein and at least one portion of fruit or vegetables—look up the breakfast ideas on page 134 or have fun experimenting with your own.

Serving sizes

This is where a lot of people go wrong with their diet, for most of us were brought up being told, "You must finish what is on your plate." However, now is your chance to rebel, as there really is no need to keep eating once you are full.

Having said that, it is best not to put temptation in the way at all. Portion sizes seem to be getting bigger all the time, especially in restaurants, and it is definitely worth seeing if you can reduce them. Everything, even healthful food, is fattening when eaten to excess, as it provides fuel that the body simply can't burn. Be especially careful of overloading on carbs, and make sure that your salad or vegetable portion is double the size of your accompanying meat/fish and potato/rice/pasta portion.

We all habitually wolf down our food these days and are often unconscious of what we are eating. Unsurprisingly, this is not good for us. It is important to eat slowly, as it takes time for the stomach to register that it is full and then send this information to the brain. Eat slowly, and you won't consume more than you want or need.

Good fats *v.* bad fats

People tend to get very confused with the whole fat issue. They may cut fat out of their diet altogether in their pursuit of a slimmer physique, but this is actually a mistake, as we need certain types of fat—some essential vitamins are soluble only in fat, and essential fatty acids, found in oily fish, avocados, seeds, and nuts, are good for brain function and healthy joints and protect against heart disease. We also need the good fats to help our body metabolize the bad fats, so that they really can help in our weight-loss quest.

The crucial distinction is therefore between the good and the bad fats. The latter are saturated fats, which come mainly from meat, dairy products, pastry, fried food, cakes, and cookies. Saturated fats are usually solid at room temperature, but they are harder to spot when they are in processed foods, so always look at the label to check how much of the fat content is "saturated."

Good fats are "monounsaturated" or essential fatty acids (omega-3 and omega-6) .

They generally come from vegetable sources such as olives, corn, avocados, and nuts, but also from fish. However, when you think about increasing your intake of healthful fats, be careful that you don't increase the amount of fat in your diet overall—all fat, whether it is in a bacon, lettuce, and tomato sandwich or an avocado salad, is still fattening.

Which carbohydrates?

Carbohydrates provide us with instaneous fuel, for when they are digested they are converted into glucose in the blood. However, different carbohydrates supply fuel in slightly different ways, and this is due to the impact that their glucose has on blood-sugar levels—known as the glycemic index (GI).

High-GI foods cause your blood-sugar levels to rocket, which provokes an immediate release of insulin to remove this sugar quickly from the bloodstream. The speed of this response is very quick and is experienced by the body as an energy crash. In order to keep your blood-sugar levels stable it is therefore a good idea to eat foods that stimulate a more moderate insulin response. Try to get most of your carbs from fruit and vegetable sources, then wholegrain and unrefined foods (such as brown rice, bread, and pasta, potatoes, lentils, and so on) and cut down on sugary and refined foods like white bread, sugar-coated cereals, candy, and cakes, which are full of calories and have almost zero nutritional value.

Keep a food diary

When planning a change in diet, it is always a good idea to take a closer look at what you are currently eating.

Keep a food diary for a week before making any changes so that you can analyze where you are going wrong. Write down absolutely everything that you eat, as you will then see in black and white what you usually subconsciously don't count.

Eat regularly

Eating regularly is an important part of losing weight, for if you skip a meal, your body will go into "starvation mode" and store any food you then give it by slowing down your metabolic rate in case it faces starvation again. However, when you eat regularly your body learns to trust that the energy from each meal can be "used up," as there will be another on its way soon.

Experiment

As part of your healthy eating plan you should experiment with some new foods. Variety in your diet is not only good for your body but essential to your motivation. Over time, you will gather more ideas, and planning meals will become easier, but on the following pages I have suggested a few recipes to get you started. There are lots of mouthwatering healthy-eating recipe books to give you more ideas and the Internet is also an invaluable resource.

Recipes

Breakfasts

BLUEBERRY AND PINEAPPLE SMOOTHIE

Blueberries are a lovely summer fruit, and they're very low in calories and very high in nutrition, providing vitamin C, iron, carbohydrates, fiber, and also potassium and magnesium.
Serves 3–4

1 cup blueberries
1 medium banana, peeled and roughly chopped
3/4 cup unsweetened pineapple juice
1 tablespoon clear honey
3 tablespoons low-fat natural yogurt

Simply put all the ingredients in a blender and process until smooth. Test for sweetness and then pour into large glasses and serve.

Nutrition info. (per serving)
123 calories

CINNAMON AND VANILLA FRENCH TOAST

This classic recipe is delicious and great for a weekend treat. Serve with a glass of fruit juice to get all your food groups in.
Serves 2–4

2 egg whites and 1 whole egg
1/2 cup skim milk
1 tablespoon vanilla extract
1 teaspoon ground cinnamon plus extra cinnamon for sprinkling
4 slices wholewheat bread
spray oil for frying

Lightly spray a large skillet, with oil and warm over a low heat. Whisk together the egg, milk, vanilla extract, and cinnamon in a bowl and then soak each slice of bread in the mixture until moist.

Fry the bread in the pan until the bottom side is golden brown, then turn over to repeat on the other side. Once the bread is sufficiently toasted, serve warm with cinnamon sprinkled over the top.

Nutrition info. (per serving)
120 calories
3.5g fat

FRUITY BREAKFAST KICK-START

This will provide the best possible start to your day and fill you up until lunchtime.

Serves 3–4

2 cups low-fat Greek yogurt
4 teaspoons clear honey
1 cup raspberries
1/2 cup blueberries
2 peaches, sliced into wedges
3/4 cup granola

Divide the yogurt between the serving dishes and drizzle over the honey. Pile fresh fruit on top and sprinkle with the muesli. Serve immediately.

Nutrition info. (per serving)
189 calories
5g fat

Lunches

BEAN AND VEGETABLE SOUP

This soup is great for a low-fat nutritional lunch.

Serves 6

Spray olive oil
1 large onion, minced
1 large carrot, minced
2 celery stalks, minced
4 small tomatoes, peeled and chopped
2 garlic cloves, minced
4 cups canned cannellini or haricot beans, drained and rinsed
1 1/4 quarts water
1 tablespoon fresh mint, chopped
1 teaspoon fresh thyme, chopped
grated rind of 1/2 lemon
1 zucchini, finely chopped
salt and freshly ground black pepper

Heat the oil in a large saucepan over medium heat and fry the onion until soft. Add the carrot, celery, tomatoes, and garlic and cook for 3–4 minutes.

Now add the beans and the water. Bring to the boil, cover, and simmer for 15 minutes. Add the herbs, lemon rind, and zucchini and season to taste. Cover and continue to simmer for 35 minutes or until the vegetables are tender.

Remove the pan from the heat and allow the mixture to cool slightly. Transfer half of the mixture into a food processor and blend until smooth. Then mix it back in with the remaining soup, heat through, and serve into slightly warmed bowls.

Nutrition info. (per serving)
109 calories
3g fat

BEET, BEAN, AND FETA SALAD

Green beans are an excellent source of bone-building calcium, and the red pigment in beets is prized for its anti-cancer agents.

Serves 4–6

6 oz. small beets, sliced
7 oz. green beans, cooked, refreshed and sliced
3 tablespoons olive oil
1 tablespoon white wine vinegar
a pinch of mustard powder
a pinch of sugar
salt and freshly ground black pepper
$3^{1}/_{2}$ oz. Greek feta cheese, crumbled

Arrange the beets and beans on a plate. In a screw-top jar, combine the oil, vinegar, mustard, sugar, and seasoning and use to dress the salad. Sprinkle the crumbled feta on top.

Nutrition info. (per serving)
83 calories
5g fat

EXOTIC SHRIMP SALAD WITH LEMON CHIVE DRESSING

This very easy, fresh-tasting salad is heaped with nutrition—the shrimp alone are a good source of protein and omega-3 fatty acids and they're also a great way to stock up on iron, zinc and vitamin E.
Serves 4

1 large papaya, halved, peeled, and cubed
4 kiwi fruit, peeled and cubed
3/4 cup strawberries, halved
14 oz. cooked peeled shrimp
juice of 1 lemon
1 tablespoon chives, minced

Combine the fruit and shrimp in a roomy salad bowl. Pour the lemon juice over the ingredients and sprinkle the chives on top. Chill for 10 minutes, then serve with crunchy green salad leaves.

Nutrition info. (per serving)
172 calories
1g fat

Main meals

TUNA STEAK WITH BLACK BEAN SALSA

This tasty salsa brings an extra zing to tuna and goes well with other fish and white meat, too.
Serves 4

5/8 cup dried black beans, soaked overnight in cold water, rinsed, and drained
5 oz. tomatoes, peeled, deseeded, and finely chopped
2 tablespoons cilantro, chopped
1 tablespoon lime juice
½ fresh red chili, deseeded and finely chopped
1 garlic clove, minced
1 tablespoon olive oil
salt and freshly ground black pepper
4 fresh tuna steaks

Put the beans in a saucepan and cover with water. Bring to the boil and cook for 10 minutes, removing any foam from the surface of the water. Reduce the heat and simmer for 1 hour until the beans are soft.

Place the beans with the tomatoes into a mixing bowl and stir in the cilantro, lime juice, chili, garlic, and half of the olive oil. Season with salt and black pepper, then set aside to marinate for about an hour.

Heat the remaining olive oil in a skillet and fry the tuna on a high heat for 2–3 minutes on each side.

Serve with the salsa and a mixed side salad.

Nutrition info. (per serving)
260 calories
10g fat

CHICKEN TANDOORI

This aromatic Indian treat lets you indulge in all the flavor of a take-out tandoori but with none of the fats, sugars, and other dieting no-nos!

Serves 4

1 lb. 3 oz. boneless, skinless chicken breasts, cut into 1 in.-thick slices
2 garlic cloves, crushed
5/8 cup low-fat natural yogurt
1 tablespoon lemon juice
1 teaspoon fresh gingerroot, grated
large pinch of chili powder (cayenne pepper)
1 teaspoon ground coriander
1 teaspoon ground cumin
½ teaspoon ground turmeric

Place the chicken in a shallow ovenproof dish and cover with the garlic, yogurt, lemon juice, and spices. Cover with plastic wrap and marinate in the refrigerator for at least 1 hour.

Preheat the oven to 400°F. Bake the chicken in the marinade for 35 minutes, stirring once or twice during cooking.

Alternatively, thread the chicken onto skewers with chunks of red onion and cook in a hot broiler for 15–20 minutes. Serve with a green salad, or brown rice or pita bread for a more substantial meal. It is delicious with minty chutney.

Nutrition info. (per serving)

175 calories
3g fat

MOROCCAN COUSCOUS WITH SPICY TOMATO SAUCE AND ROASTED CAULIFLOWER

Couscous has a low GI rating and therefore helps to maintain stable blood-sugar levels. It's also a good source of dietary fiber and protects against digestive disorders and disease. Serves 4

1 cauliflower, broken into florets
2 tablespoons olive oil
grated rind and juice of 2 lemons
1 garlic clove
1 whole bird's-eye chili pepper
1 tablespoon fresh cilantro, leaves and stalks
1 red onion
3/4-in. piece fresh gingerroot, peeled
1 teaspoon cumin seeds, toasted
1 teaspoon coriander seeds, toasted
1 teaspoon ground turmeric
1 teaspoon tomato paste
14 oz. chopped tomatoes
1 bay leaf
salt and freshly ground black pepper
5/8 cup dried apricots, roughly chopped
2 tablespoons fresh mint, chopped
1 1/3 cups couscous
1 tablespoon flat leaf parsley, chopped

Preheat the oven to 425°F. Place the cauliflower on a baking tray, sprinkle with 1 tablespoon of the olive oil, and roast for 20 minutes, turning once.

In a food processor, blend the rind and juice of 1 of the lemons, the garlic, chili, coriander, onion, and ginger to a smooth paste. Then heat the remaining oil in a skillet and cook the paste gently for 10 minutes. Grind the toasted seeds together to a fine powder and add to the skillet along with the turmeric, tomato paste, chopped tomatoes, and bay leaf. Cook for 20 minutes, then discard the bay leaf, season to taste, and add the mint and apricots.

Place the couscous in a bowl, cover with cold water, and leave for 20 minutes until the water is absorbed. To warm through, place in a strainer over a pan of boiling water for 5 minutes, then stir in the remaining lemon, the flat-leaf parsley, and seasoning. To serve, place the couscous in a dish, add the roasted cauliflower, and pour the spicy tomato sauce over.

Nutrition info. (per serving)
339 calories
10g fat

Desserts

CANTELOUPE SORBET

This deliciously refreshing sorbet is just the thing after a hot and energetic uphill walk. Serves 10

1 cup fine granulated sugar
1 cup water
1 canteloupe, halved and cut into chunks
1 tablespoon lemon juice
strawberries or tropical fruit

Put the sugar and water together in a saucepan and dissolve over a low heat. Then bring to the boil and simmer for 3 minutes. Leave to cool.

Place the melon flesh, lemon juice, and sugar syrup in a food processor and blend for 1 minute or until smooth.

Either place in a suitable container and put in the freezer for 3 hours, stirring occasionally to break up the ice crystals, or freeze in an ice-cream machine.

Nutrition info. (per serving)
135 calories

BANANA RICE PUDDING

This feels much naughtier than it really is! Serves 6

scant 1/3 cup short grain pudding rice
2 1/2 cups low-fat milk
3 drops vanilla extract
3 tablespoons honey
2 bananas, peeled and sliced thinly
zest of 1/2 lemon, finely grated
2 egg whites

Heat the oven to 440°F. Place the rice, milk, vanilla extract, and honey in a saucepan and bring to the boil. Reduce the heat and allow to simmer for 1 hour, or until the rice is soft.

Mix the bananas into the rice with the lemon zest. Whisk the egg whites until stiff and fold into the rice. Spoon the mixture into an ovenproof dish and bake in the oven for 25–30 mins., until golden brown.

Nutrition info. (per serving)
186 calories
2g fat

Resources

Collage Video
www.collagevideo.com/exercise
800-433-6769
Exercise videos and DVDs, also music for walking

Cross Country International: Walking Vacations
www.walkingvacations.com
800-828-8768
Hiking trips in the U.S., Australia, and Europe

ENELL Sports Bras
www.enell.com
Specialists in larger sizes

FATFREE: The Low Fat Vegetarian Recipe Archive
www.fatfree.com
Thousands of healthful recipes

Fitmed Inc.
www.heartmonitors.com
800-959-4089
Heart rate monitors and other fitness accessories

Leave No Trace Center for Outdoor Ethics
www.lnt.org
Nonprofit organization dedicated to promoting and inspiring outdoor recreation

Living and Raw Foods
www.livingfoods.com
Great recipes and information on vegetarian foods

Low Fat Lifestyle
www.lowfatlifestyle.com
Tips on cooking healthful meals and ordering wisely when dining out; list of 20 fast-food chains with menu items analyzed for calories and nutritional content

Low-fat Recipes
www.low-fat-recipes.com
Nutrition advice and cookbooks

National Heart, Lung and Blood Institute
www.nhlbisupport.com
301-592-8573
Part of the National Institutes of Health; web site includes calculation of body mass index

New England Hiking Holidays
www.nehikingholidays.com
800-869-0949
Not just in New England—walking trips in many parts of the U.S. and abroad, too

Peak to Peak
www.peaktopeak.net
Links to hundreds of hiking clubs all over the U.S. and some abroad

Pro-Form
www.proform.com
Heart rate monitors, treadmills, exercise mats, and other equipment and accessories for walkers

SkiWalking
www.skiwalking.com
231-334-3080
Information on Nordic walking, along with poles, accessories, and DVD

U.S. Department of Agriculture
www.usda.gov
Information on food quality, labeling, dietary health

Walker's Warehouse
www.walkerswarehouse.com/fitness
888-972-9255
Footwear, clothing, accessories for fitness activities

Walk 4 Life
www.walk4life.com
Specialists in pedometers

The Walking Site
www.thewalkingsite.com
Charity walks, walking clubs, shopping for books, videos and DVDs

NB All this information is relevant at time of going to print but web site content may change and become out of date.

Index

Acknowledgments

A massive "thank you" to all my family and friends for their constant support and advice. I appreciate how fortunate I am to have such remarkable people in my life.

Thanks to you all for the different parts you have played in the creation of this book, and to my colleagues, teachers, and clients along the way, from whom I have learned so much.

A special thanks to my partner, Ken, who continues to give me direction, support, and love and, more importantly, is the one who understands.

Thanks also to my publisher, Kyle Cathie, and to my editor Vicki Murrell, photographer Guy Hearn, model Juliet Murrell, and designer Caroline Hillier.

Thanks to USA Pro for continuing to support me with their fantastic clothing.

Additional photography credits: page 10 Stockbyte Platinum / Alamy, 49 (top) image100 / Alamy, (bottom) Ty Allison / Getty Images, 55 Westend61 / Alamy, 56 Profimedia International s.r.o / Alamy, 57 Stefan Schuetz / Getty Images, 59 Steve Casimiro / Getty Images, 61 Stefan Schuetz / zefa / Corbis, 62 Jennie Hart / Alamy, 63 Photofusion Picture Library / Alamy, 64 Miguel Riopa / Getty Images, 112 Swerve / Alamy, 113 Mode Images Limited / Alamy